CU00656231

ANGLESEY AIR ACCIDENTS

ANGLESEY AIR ACCIDENTS
during the Twentieth Century

Roy Sloan

© *Text: Roy Sloan*

Copyright © by Gwasg Carreg Gwalch 2001.
All rights reserved. No part of this publication may be reproduced
or transmitted, in any form or by any means, without permission.

The publishers wish to acknowledge the financial
aid of Elizabeth Zollihofer for printing and reproducing
the photograph sections of this book.

ISBN: 0-86381-677-0

Cover design: Sian Parri

First published in 2001 by
Gwasg Carreg Gwalch, 12 Iard yr Orsaf, Llanrwst, Wales LL26 0EH
✆ *01492 642031* 🖷 *01492 641502*
✆ *books@carreg-gwalch.co.uk Internet: www.carreg-gwalch.co.uk*

The Author
Born in 1945, Roy Sloan is a native of Anglesey, where he now resides. He is employed as a careers information officer at the University of Wales, Bangor. Apart from aviation his other interests include music, photography and mountaineering.

Other books by Roy Sloan:

Early Aviation in North Wales, Gwasg Carreg Gwalch, £2.75

Wings of War over Gwynedd, Gwasg Carreg Gwalch, £4.50

Aircraft Crashes – flying accidents in Gwynedd, 1910-1990, Gwasg Carreg Gwalch, £5.50

The Tale of Tabun – Nazi Chemical Weapons in North Wales, Gwasg Carreg Gwalch, £5.95

Contents

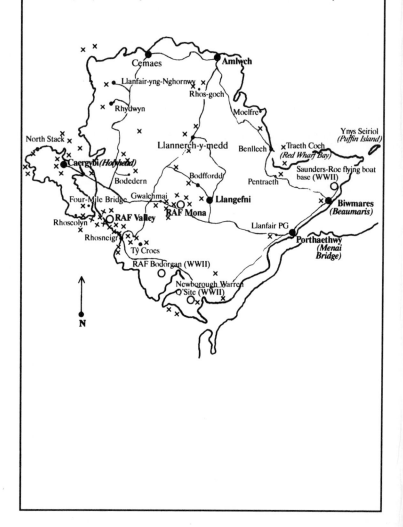

Aircraft crash sites, Anglesey
(only the major accident locations are indicated)

Cemaes

Amlwch

Llanfair-yng-Nghornwy

Rhos-goch

Rhydwyn

Moelfre

North Stack

Ynys Seiriol
(Puffin Island)

Llannerch-y-medd

Benllech

Caergybi *(Holyhead)*

Traeth Coch
(Red Wharf Bay)

Bodedern

Bodffordd

Saunders-Roc flying boat
base (WWII)

Pentraeth

Four-Mile Bridge

Gwalchmai

Llangefni

Biwmares
(Beaumaris)

Rhoscolyn

RAF Valley

RAF Mona

Rhosneigr

Llanfair PG

Porthaethwy
*(Menai
Bridge)*

Tŷ Croes

RAF Bodorgan (WWII)

Newborough Warren
'Site (WWII)

N

Introduction and Acknowledgements

The air has been described, somewhat poetically, as 'a limitless ocean which flows to every man's door' but though always life-giving to those on the ground, to anyone who ventures upon the aerial currents of this ocean it has a dangerous perfidy. Like the sea, the air is, and always will be a treacherous element – indeed, as treacherous and unforgiving as a jilted lover. It is this unforgiving aspect of the air which creates many of the risks of aviation. Perhaps the major difference between flying and other forms of transport is the level of commitment that is intrinsic in the act of becoming airborne. By stepping into an aircraft, whether it be the mightiest jet or a humble microlight, the occupant will have entrusted himself or herslf, body and soul, to that machine and its correct functioning.

Only a military pilot strapped in an ejection seat has the luxury of knowing there is an excellent chance of escape in an emergency. For the rest of those who fly, whether frequently or infrequently, whether a nervous passenger embarking upon a first flight or an experienced pilot with thousands of hours entered in his log book, the individual's fate is inextricably linked with the aircraft that person happens to be flying in.

In an ideal world the air would be totally benign and aircraft would be perfectly safe and there would be no accidents but we know that a perfectly safe aircraft has never and can never be built. Therefore we have to live with the reality of the risks arising from aviation. The causes of flying accidents are many and varied: bad weather, airframe defects and failures, design faults, engine failure, human errors, physical incapacitation, bird strikes etc. These factors are universal, with many of them, either singly or in combination, being responsible for the incidents that have occurred in Anglesey. If one cares to examine the island's aviation history during the twentieth century, it does not take long or detailed scrutiny to realise that it can be divided into three clear and distinct periods: before, during and after the Second World War. Before the War there was hardly any aviation to speak of, during the War there was a *tremendous* amount and after the War there was still quite a lot but not as much as before. That, in a nutshell, is the history of aviation in Anglesey.

However, in order to provide the reader with some background to the accidents described in this book, a little more detail is required and so it is worth looking, albeit very briefly, at those three historical periods. During the first period, from 1910 until 1939, the only activity of any significance (besides the pioneering flights of Robert Loraine, described in Chapter 1) was the establishment by the Royal Naval Air Service (RNAS) of an airship station, in 1915, on a site in the middle of the island, a few miles from the town of Llangefni. This station, named RNAS Llangefni, operated a number of small non-rigid airships, or 'blimps' as they were known, on anti-submarine patrols in the Irish Sea and Mersey approaches, the submarines in question being, of course, German U-boats. During the First World War their presence in British coastal waters represented a growing and potentially serious threat to shipping, hence the decision to introduce airship patrols in an attempt to counter the threat. The Anglesey station was one of many others in the UK and was active until the end of the war in 1918.

After the RNAS 'blimps' disappeared from the skies of Anglesey, the island's aviation activity more or less came to a standstill and remained so until the massive jolt of the Second World War provided an impetus for development. The war brought about the establishment of three military airfields on Anglesey soil – RAFs Valley, Mona and Bodorgan. By far the most important was Valley. Opened in February 1941 as one of Fighter Command's stations, this airfield became an additional base, to those already in existence, for the provision of fighter defences in the north west and Merseyside. It was intended that Valley should have one day fighter and one night fighter squadron in residence, the first occupants in the former category being a detachment of Hurricanes from 312 (Czech) Squadron in March. To provide night fighter cover, No.456 (RAAF) Squadron was formed at Valley in June 1941. Equipped with Beaufighters, the squadron suffered a number of accidents, some of which are described in Chapters 6 and 10. In the summer of 1943 Valley underwent a radical change. With enemy activity non-existent by that summer the base lost its role as a fighter station and became a terminal for American heavy bombers crossing the Atlantic to join operational squadrons in England. At the end of the war the flow of traffic was reversed and all the B-17s and B-24s, over 2,000 in number, returned to the US via Valley.

The second of Anglesey's airfields, RAF Mona, was built during 1942 on the site of RNAS Llangefni, the airship station dating from the First World War. Mona was to be an aircrew training airfield and during December 1942 No.3 Air Gunnery School took up residence. The School was equipped with mostly obsolete aircraft, Bothas and Battles. This unit departed in November 1943 and was replaced by No.8 (Observers) Advanced Flying Unit, formed at Mona. Its role was to extend the usefulness of Observers by training them in other aircrew duties such as radio operation, air gunnery, navigation and bomb aiming. Ansons were the only type of aircraft flown. The unit was disbanded in June 1945.

The third airfield built in Anglesey was RAF Bodorgan. It also happened to be the smallest and least important of the three. Bodorgan's main task was the unglamorous job of army co-operation, providing aerial targets, in the form of towed drogues and pilotless drones, for Royal Artillery gunners at the nearby camp of Tŷ Croes. The drogue targets were towed by Hawker Henleys and Miles Martinets whilst the drones were radio-controlled variants of the Tiger Moth, known as Queen Bees.

The fourth aviation development seen on the island during the war years was the construction of a flying boat base near Beaumaris by the firm of Saunders-Roe Ltd. In 1940 German air raids on the company's headquarters and factory at Cowes, in the Isle of Wight, were causing great disruption, forcing Saunders-Roe to move to a safer area, away from southern England. After an extensive search of coastal areas in the north west they chose a site near Beaumaris, where a house known as Friars was for sale, together with fifty acres of land fronting the Menai Strait. It was an ideal site for flying boat operations. The land was purchased and soon hangars and buildings were erected upon it. The most important work carried out by Saunders-Roe at Beaumaris was the conversion of American-built Consolidated Catalina flying boats to meet the RAF's operational requirements. These aircraft were ferried across the Atlantic to Anglesey, where the conversion work was done, after which the 'Cats', as they were known, were delivered to operational squadrons within Coastal Command. Over 300 Catalinas were converted at Beaumaris during the war.

From Valley, Mona, Bodorgan and Beaumaris innumerable flights took place during the war years. In comparison to what had gone before, this was a veritable explosion of activity. Almost overnight what was, from an aviation viewpoint, a desert, had been transformed into a lush, fruitful landscape filled with runways, hangars, hardstandings, control towers, windsocks and most importantly of all, aeroplanes aplenty. Whereas previously, local skies were more or less devoid of aircraft, now machines of many different types criss-crossed the island's airspace almost continuously. However, the downside of this enormous increase in flying was a correspondingly large increase in accidents. Such events, once an extreme rarity, became commonplace with occasions when there would be multiple crashes – two, or even three in a day.

Then, once the war was over so aerial activity in Anglesey declined dramatically, along with many other parts of the country. In 1945 none of the island's three airfields were regarded as having any further operational purpose and were put on what the RAF called a Care and Maintenance basis pending firm decisions on their future. In the event, Bodorgan closed completely and reverted to agriculture, Mona remained on 'hold' and was used for non-aviation purposes whilst Valley saw some minor activity during the latter half of the 1940s – the very nadir of its existence, in fact. Meanwhile, at Beaumaris Saunders-Roe had, after the war came to an end, abandoned aviation operations for other forms of manufacture, such as the construction of torpedo boats for the Navy.

The third period of Anglesey's aviation history dates from 1951, with the emergence of Valley from the post-war doldrums. It was to become the home of No.202 Advanced Flying School (AFS) whose task was to convert piston trained pilots to jet flying. The School was equipped with Meteor T.7s and Vampire FB5s. Later, Vampire T.11s were operated. In June 1954 202 AFS was disbanded and No.7 Flying Training School (FTS) reformed at Valley. There was an additional task; that of training Royal Navy pilots. In 1958 this commitment was transferred to Linton-on-Ouse and Valley took over from Worksop the task, carried out by No.4 FTS, of providing advanced fast-jet training of RAF pilots. But it was not until 1960 that 4FTS reformed at Valley to replace 7FTS. In 1962 the unit's Vampires were replaced by Hawker Siddeley Gnats and in 1967 the Gnats were supplemented by a squadron of Hawker Hunters. The Gnat era lasted until 1976 when a new training aircraft entered service with 4FTS. This was the immensely successful British Aerospace Hawk, arguably the best jet trainer ever built, and sold by British Aerospace not only to the RAF but also fourteen other air forces throughout the world.

An interesting development and one of great consequence for North Wales generally was the establishment, in 1955, of a Search and Rescue (SAR) unit at Valley. This was 'C' Flight of 22 Squadron. Equipped with Whirlwind helicopters, the unit flew these machines until 1976 when they were replaced by the Wessex, which in turn was replaced by Sea Kings in 1997. Whilst 'C' Flight's official role was to rescue aircrew from military aircraft that had crashed, missions to rescue civilians from a variety of predicaments were also flown. Indeed, these latter types of missions soon came to dominate the unit's work. In the main, those who needed rescuing were either amateur yachtsmen or climbers and walkers in the mountains of Snowdonia. Since 1955 the yellow helicopters of RAF Valley have become a familiar sight in the skies of North Wales and the reader will find these 'whirlybirds' and their humanitarian role mentioned in many chapters of the present volume.

As regards RAF Mona, alongside the revival of Valley's fortunes in 1951, this mid-Anglesey airfield was resurrected to the somewhat humble status of Relief Landing Ground for Valley. Its single runway is still used for 'roller' landings to this day. In the mid-1970s Mona became the home of a civilian flying club. The club flourished and continues to do so.

The return of regular flying activity to the island in 1951 meant that accidents returned also but on nothing like the scale seen previously. What were at one time weekly or monthly events now became much sparser and crashes resulting in serious injury or death decreased to one or two annually. Looking at the century as a whole, there have been eighty-six military and six civilian fatalities in Anglesey as a result of flying accidents, the frequency of their occurrence corresponding closely to the three widely differing historical periods already referred to; only one death before 1940, sixty-one deaths during the Second World War and thirty in the latter half of the century. We can see at a glance that most of these fatalities took place between 1940 and 1945, representing two-thirds of the total and reflecting the intense operational activity which so characterised those strife-torn years.

The wartime figure includes the four *Luftwaffe* members who lost their lives as a result of being shot down by an RAF fighter but excludes the eleven men who drowned attempting to rescue the crew of a Botha which crashed in the sea off Rhosneigr in August 1941. This exclusion is made because the eleven unfortunate men did not die as a direct result of the accident. Their deaths only came about when rescue attempts failed. For the same reason, this tragic tale of heroism is omitted from the present volume because it is outside the book's scope.

The Appendix lists a total of 172 accidents which have occurred in Anglesey during the twentieth century. It is not a definitive list and includes only the most serious or noteworthy accidents. Of these, over fifty are briefly described in the text whilst the stories of twenty-three others are narrated in full. They range from the mishaps befalling Robert Loraine's 'stick and string' biplane of 1910 to the relatively few crashes involving the modern, technologically sophisticated jets operating from RAF Valley in the 1980s and 1990s. More detailed descriptions of some of these accidents can be found in my earlier volume, *Aircraft Crashes in Gwynedd 1910-1990* (Gwasg Carreg Gwalch, 1994).

Since the days of my boyhood in the 1950s and wonderfully memorable trips to RAF Valley's Open Days – trips which had the result of creating within me a lifelong fascination with aircraft – I have observed the aviation scene in Anglesey with a great deal of interest and pleasure. Only on one occasion, however, have I actually seen an aircraft in trouble, the circumstances of which are described in Chapter 16. Though nobody was killed in the accident, nevertheless, it was not pleasant to witness and it was my most fervent wish and still remains so, that I will not have to witness anything similar again.

As regards crash sites in Anglesey, it is important to stress that those accidents which did not happen on airfields or in coastal waters were all on private land and that no access is possible. Even more importantly, not a trace of wreckage remains at any of these sites to tempt souvenir hunters.

Finally, I would like to thank all those individuals who have been kind enough to provide me with help in the course of my researches, not only as far as the present volume is concerned but my other works also. Meeting so many people who have charmed and delighted me, and some of whom have become firm friends, has been one of the most rewarding and stimulating aspects of my research into local aviation history. I wish to mention in particular Myrddin ap Dafydd of Gwasg Carreg Gwalch for all his guidance and supportiveness, John Cave, David Earl, Geraint Ellis, my good friend Arthur Evans, Eric Hughes, Stephen Hutton, R. Islwyn James, Dr J. Janssen, head of the Royal Netherlands Air Force History Unit, Arthur Jones, Bob Jones of RAF Valley's meteorological office, Christiana Jones, Ellis Wyn Jones, Jack Jones, William Hugh Jones, J.J. Koppe of the Museum of Military Aviation, Soesterberg, Netherlands, Group Captain (Retd) Philip Langrill, the late Jack Leaversuch, Squadron Leader (Retd) Daniel Lockyer, Joan Loraine, Brendan Maguire, Flight Lieutenant (Retd) Douglas Mee, Herrick Moseley, Ernest Naish, Idris Owen, Owen Pritchard, Richard Radcliffe, Geoffrey Siers, Group Captain (Retd) Mike Smith, Squadron Leader David Ward of the RAF Inspectorate of Flight Safety, David Watkins, Elisabeth Wegener Sleeswijk and Hugh Williams. Many thanks also to those who have contributed information but who have expressed a wish to remain anonymous. My debt of gratitude to everyone who has given me help is profound.

Roy Sloan
Brynsiencyn, 2000

Abbreviations

AI	Airborne Interception radar
ATC	Air Traffic Control
CAA	Civil Aviation Authority
CAM	Catapult Aircraft Merchant (ship)
CFS	Central Flying School
CO	Commanding Officer
ETA	Estimated Time of Arrival
FTS	Flying Training School
h.p.	horse power
IMC	Instrument Meteorological Conditions
MoD	Ministry of Defence
MoD (AFD)	Ministry of Defence, Air Force Department
MT	Mechanical Transport
MU	Maintenance Unit
NCO	Non Commissioned Officer
(O)AFU	(Observers) Advanced Flying Unit
OTU	Operational Training Unit
PIO	Pilot Induced Oscillation
QFI	Qualified Flying Instructor
RA	Royal Artillery
RAAF	Royal Australian Air Force
RFC	Royal Flying Corps
RN	Royal Navy
RNAS	Royal Naval Air Service
RNVR	Royal Naval Volunteer Reserve
RO	Radio Operator
rpm	revolutions per minute
SAR	Search and Rescue
SHQ	Station Headquarters
SMO	Senior Medical Officer
SPTU	Staff Pilots Training Unit
SSQ	Station Sick Quarters
TASF	Transit Aircraft Servicing Flight

USAAF   United States Army Air Force
VMC   Visual Meteorological Conditions

1

Pioneering Flights & Mishaps

On Wednesday, 10 August 1910 the pioneer aviator Robert Loraine flew his Farman biplane from Blackpool along the North Wales coast to Anglesey, thus earning for himself the distinction of becoming the first airman to fly in Wales. He was also destined to become the first to crash in the region!

Loraine had a strong, though complex personality – energetic, decisive and with a love of adventure, yet possessed also of a highly developed artistic sensitivity. He was rich and well-known, with a considerable reputation as an actor-manager and could count no less a person than the great playwright and critic, George Bernard Shaw, amongst his closest friends. Indeed the childless Shaw regarded him as a surrogate son. During the early years of the century, Loraine had toured the United States in Shaw's play *Man & Superman*, a tour which netted the actor-manager a personal fortune of £40,000, money that was later used with almost reckless abandon to finance his flying exploits, including those located in Anglesey.

In 1909 he witnessed Louis Bleriot's crossing by air of the English Channel and the fame this flight brought Bleriot made a deep impression upon Loraine. He decided that he too would fly, and become a pilot-hero. In April 1910, at the age of thirty-four, he went to France to enroll at Bleriot's flying school and then at the Henry Farman school, where, in June, he gained his pilot's certificate, though at huge expense. One of the conditions imposed upon him during his period of training was that he had to pay for any damage caused to the school's machines – and damage there certainly was. The route to his pilot's *brevet* was littered with the wreckage of broken aircraft but Loraine's enthusiasm remained undimmed by his mishaps and he was content to foot a substantial repair bill.

Before he left the Farman school he purchased one of their racing biplanes, at a cost of £7,000 – a huge sum of money in 1910 and indicative of the fact that aviation was then a rich man's activity. This biplane was later to spend a not inconsiderable amount of time on Anglesey soil, there to suffer many grievous injuries at the somewhat inexpert hands of its pilot. To maintain his new purchase in proper working order Loraine needed a mechanic and so he promptly enticed the Farman school's chief mechanic, Jules Vedrines, an aggressive (and vehemently Anglophobe) Parisian, away from his employers into his (Loraine's) employ at the enormous salary, for those days, of £150 per month, plus expenses. Vedrines, like the aircraft that was in his charge, was also destined to spend time in Anglesey during August and September, 1910. This experience led him to form an even lower opinion of the island's good Welsh people than he had of the English; 'One knows the English are beasts', he was heard to say, 'but here the people are savages' – a typically caustic comment from the mechanic's lips.

Loraine, after gaining his 'wings', lost no time in making public appearances in his new role of aviator. He made good flights at the Bournemouth Flying Meeting in July, followed by attendance at a similar event held at Blackpool during the following month. It was at this second meeting that he conceived the idea of attempting an over-water flight of sixty miles across the Irish Sea, from Holyhead to Dublin, which if successful, would be a world record for a flight of this type. As the fiery Vedrines remarked, 'he had great ideas, always big ideas, and that is what counts in our little Science of Aviation.'

While the Irish Sea crossing was undoubtedly a big idea, it was also a dangerous one, because an over-water flight of any length was risky: aircraft were primitive, aerial navigation was at a rudimentary stage and worst of all, aero-engines of that period were notoriously unreliable. Therefore, the possibility of being forced to ditch because of engine failure was high. Once in the water, a downed pilot's chances of quick rescue were slim, as personal survival equipment was undeveloped while sophisticated search and rescue techniques lay many decades in the future.

But consideration of the hazards involved in the flight did not bother the would-be conqueror of the Irish Sea overmuch. Having got a trusted friend, ex-soldier and playwright Captain George Smart, to make all the necessary arrangements at Holyhead, Loraine took the opportunity afforded by the fine weather of Wednesday, 10 August and left Blackpool at 6.30 a.m. in his Farman biplane, with the intention of flying along the North Wales coast until he reached his destination. Following in a car was Vedrines, accompanied by his brother Emil, who had come over to Britain to provide assistance and companionship to Jules, who, ever the Anglophobe, had found himself excessively burdened by loneliness in a land whose inhabitants he regarded, as we have seen, with the deepest suspicion.

Loraine's flight to Holyhead did not go to plan, however. Emil Vedrines, who lacked his brother's skills and who should never have been allowed to touch the Farman, had, most unfortunately, rigged the biplane's controls incorrectly that morning and though the machine flew as it should, an enormous amount of strain was imposed not only upon the control cables but also the pilot's nerves. While approaching Colwyn Bay, at 8.00 a.m., he decided to make a precautionary landing on the invitingly smooth grass of Rhos-on-Sea golf links. By virtue of this flight he became the first airman to fly in Wales. The Vedrines brothers arrived during the early afternoon and proceeded to re-rig the Farman. This time there were no mistakes and at 5.00 p.m. Loraine took off, to the accompaniment of cheers from a huge crowd of onlookers.

Reaching Holyhead should have been relatively simple, by following the railway line, for instance, which was an almost foolproof method of route-finding for even the most incompetent of navigators – but the biplane's pilot chose instead to follow the Anglesey coast, which on that day of hot sunshine was shrouded in a thick heat haze, as was the surrounding sea. The result was that Loraine became lost. Thoroughly disorientated, he wandered far out to sea, getting deeper into trouble with every passing minute. His excuse was that he fell asleep. Whether this was true or not, he was eventually roused into action and with a rapidly emptying fuel tank adding a sense of urgency to his calculations, he used the sun's position to work out an approximate course which, he hoped, would bring him to Anglesey. It did, and not a moment too soon – one mile from shore his engine stopped. Gliding earthwards, Loraine, hugely relieved at his deliverance from calamity, crossed a rocky coastline and landed in a field which, he later discovered, belonged to Bryn Goelcerth farm, near the village of Llanfairynghornwy and only seven miles, by air, from the pilot's intended destination. But in the event, those seven miles were to cost him dear. As his biographer (his wife, Winifred) noted, 'Bryn Goelcerth was to prove Robert's Golgotha.'

For two days the biplane remained at Bryn Goelcerth, grounded by strong winds which made the brief hop to Holyhead impossible. On Friday, 12 August, with the wind abating somewhat, Loraine could not suppress his impatience any longer and decided to take a chance. Willing villagers, described most uncharitably by the *Manchester Guardian* as 'weird Welsh islanders', helped roll the aircraft to the top of a slope so that a downhill run would assist the machine to become airborne. However, this advantage was nullified to some extent by the fact that the take-off was not into wind. Additionally, barring the way at the end of the run was a small hummock of fifteen feet which Loraine, struggling to gain height, attempted to clear but failed to do so and crashed. He thus became the first pilot to have a flying accident in Anglesey. This crash caused serious damage to the biplane and left it so broken that the subsequent repair was tantamount to a rebuild – a task which took the Vedrines brothers until early September to complete and for which purpose a temporary hangar was erected. Once built, the hangar and its contents became the focus of interest for practically the whole island during this period. Large numbers of people flocked to Llanfairynghornwy, all drawn by the powerful, magnetic attraction of the aircraft's presence. They came on foot, on bicycles, by charabanc, by pony and trap, a privileged few by motor-car, each with but one aim; to see for themselves the biplane – a sight few, if any, had seen before in their lives.

Meanwhile, Jules and Emil Vedrines had been hard at work repairing the Farman in its temporary shelter. The brothers, during their stay at Llanfairynghornwy, had, in a typically Gallic manner, exhibited a fondness for drink and female company – behaviour which scandalised the deeply religious Welsh community of the district. While repair work was in progress, Loraine had left Anglesey for London, where he had acting commitments but on 4 September he was back on the island, as by then his aeroplane was fully repaired and ready to take to the air.

A gentle, favourable wind was blowing and so it appeared that success might, at last, be within reach, but the flight was doomed before it began. Unfortunately, the field chosen for the take-off was reclaimed bog, which retained much of its marshy character – a fact which neither Loraine, the Vedrines brothers, George Smart or anyone else seemed to have noticed. It was to be a costly oversight. The Farman's 50 h.p. Gnome engine was started and away went the biplane, only to meet disaster within seconds; no sooner had the wheels began to rotate than they sank into the soft ground, bringing the machine's forward impetus to an abrupt halt after a mere few yards of travel. With a sharp crack, the wheels and centre section collapsed, pinning the pilot in the wreckage. Luckily he suffered nothing worse than badly bruised legs. This crash meant that Loraine was not only the victim of the first flying accident in Anglesey but the second also!

After this latest setback, the mangled aircraft, little more than a heap of splintered wood and torn fabric, was ignominiously loaded on to a humble farmcart and taken by road to Holyhead, there to be repaired yet again by the long-suffering Jules Vedrines, who worked at a truly frantic pace and completed the job within a week, allowing Loraine to become airborne on Sunday, 11 September, and embark upon his much-desired flight across the Irish Sea. Details of this flight are beyond the scope of the present volume, except to say that during the crossing the Farman's engine stopped and restarted (fortunately) no less than *five* times. But the bad luck which had bedevilled Loraine since his first landing at Llanfairynghornwy still clung to him and his aircraft as it approached the Irish coast.

Within a few miles of land, the biplane suddenly began to plunge and dip in the most alarming fashion. The rigging wire was beginning to fail, and then, a little later, two control wires broke, making the machine impossible to fly. It lost height rapidly and fell into the sea a mere 200 yards from shore, at Howth Head, to the north of Dublin Bay. At the very point when victory was, at last, within reach, it had turned into the most bitter defeat. Loraine's disappointment was profound. Because he had failed to reach land, even though it was only by a hairsbreadth, he could not claim to have completed the crossing. Nevertheless, his was a fine performance and a world record for over-water flying.

After his Anglesey misadventures, he lost much of his interest in aviation, except for one further dramatic flight; at the end of September 1910 he became the first pilot to send a wireless message from the air, as part of an experiment carried out by the War Office. During the First World War he became an excellent (non-flying) Squadron Commander, displaying first-rate qualities of leadership. As for Jules Vedrines, the chronically aggressive mechanic, he achieved a long-held ambition to become a pilot and in a meteoric rise went on to become one of France's leading aviators, winning prizes galore and breaking many records. He survived the War, during which he flew highly dangerous missions landing spies behind enemy lines, but he was killed in a flying accident in 1919 by which time he was a legendary figure in France. And as for the first flight across the Irish Sea – the record-breaking flight which Loraine had craved so much and which had been so cruelly denied him – it was finally achieved by a Rhyl-based pilot, Vivian Hewitt, on 26 April 1912, when he flew from Holyhead to Dublin in his Bleriot monoplane. Many years later, in the 1930s, Hewitt, who had become a millionaire through inherited wealth, settled at Cemlyn, on the north west coast of Anglesey, a location only two miles or so from where Loraine had made his historic landing in 1910.

Eighty years after that event, the author, who knew Loraine had three daughters, was attempting to trace them and in 1993 he succeeded, much to his satisfaction, in making contact with the middle of the three – Joan Loraine. This was particularly gratifying for the author, as Miss Loraine represented, through her father, a direct link with the very first days of aviation in Wales. In December 1994, the author approached BBC Radio Wales and suggested that they interview Miss Loraine – a suggestion to which they readily agreed. The interview was broadcast shortly before Christmas of that year. Thus, while Robert Loraine was 'in the air' in 1910, eighty-four years later his daughter was 'on the air' in Wales.

2

The First Fatality

Whilst Loraine's misadventures, described in the previous chapter, can be looked upon in an almost lighhearted manner redolent of *Those Magnificent Men in their Flying Machines* because no injuries or loss of life resulted from these misadventures, the same cannot be said of the accident which now concerns us. It was, in fact, the first fatal flying accident in Anglesey and took place during the First World War.

The date of its occurrence was 7 November 1917, but before we move on to detail the circumstances of the crash it is necessary, first of all, to provide some background information.

Aerial activity on the island from 1915 until 1918 was bound up exclusively with the fight against German submarines in the Irish Sea. As part of Britain's defensive measures to combat the threat from U-boats, anti-submarine patrols were undertaken by airships operating from various locations, usually close to the coast, in order to protect merchant shipping in the major sea areas of the UK. To cover the Irish Sea sector and the vital sea lanes leading to the port of Liverpool, the Admiralty established an airship station in Anglesey, located a few miles from the town of Llangefni, on the site of what is now RAF Mona.

From this station, a number of small airships – never more than half a dozen – crewed by men of the Royal Naval Air Service (RNAS) continuously patrolled the Irish Sea and Liverpool Bay during the period of the war. It was important work, though of a routine nature and often tedious in the extreme. The description of these airships as 'animated scarecrows' was very apt.

During the late summer and autumn of 1917, U-boat activity in the Irish Sea increased considerably, putting great pressure on the Anglesey-based airships and by early November the workload was so heavy that a request for additional resources was sent to the Admiralty. In response came a message from that august body stating that six Airco DH4 aircraft (twin seater day bombers) would be sent to assist, despite the fact that the RNAS landing ground, while perfectly adequate for airships, was far below the standard required for the very different demands of aircraft operation.

The Flight of six biplanes, powered by their 375 h.p. Rolls-Royce Eagle engines, took off on the morning of Wednesday, 7 November from their London base. All went well until they reached North Wales, where they encountered bad weather: strong winds, rain and low cloud. Four of the aircraft gave up and landed at Shotwick airfield (renamed RAF Sealand in 1924) near Queensferry, leaving the other two machines to pursue their goal. As they approached Lavan Sands (Traeth Lavan), an extensive area of sandbanks and coastal mud flats lying between Bangor and the village of Abergwyngregyn, one of the pilots looked down at Lavan's broad expanse, uncovered by a low tide, and decided that he would abandon his flight. He made a successful landing. Both he and his passenger were unhurt and tried to salvage their aircraft from the wet sand. Help was sought from two local farmers, the Pritchard brothers of Glanmor Isa* and Aber Ogwen farms. Horses were used in an attempt to remove the DH4 from the clutches of an incoming tide but because of broken tow ropes etc. progress was slow – too slow, in fact, and the aircraft was lost to the sea. Eventually, after a few days, the engine was salvaged and what remained of the fuselage set on fire.

Meanwhile, the sole remaining pilot still airborne, bravely pressed on towards Anglesey. He was 2nd Lt. Bernard Carter, RFC, the nineteen-year old son of a Gloucestershire clergyman.

*Interestingly enough, during the following year, 1918, fifty acres of land at Glanmor Isa was requisitioned and used by the newly-formed RAF as a base from where DH6 aircraft flew anti-submarine patrols in the Irish Sea. For details see the author's *Early Aviation in North Wales*, (Gwasg Carreg Gwalch, 1989).

The passenger in Carter's aircraft (serial number A7654) was a Corporal by the name of Harold Smith. To the pilot's credit he succeeded in locating the airship station at Llangefni despite the bad weather but, sadly, this feat of airmanship and navigation was to end in disaster.

An RNAS officer who happened to be watching Carter make his landing – an especially difficult one in the strong, gusting wind – becomes our witness to the fate of the young man at the machine's controls. According to the onlooker, when the DH4 was at a height of 300 feet, it turned on to its final approach but did so rather sharply. At the same moment, the aircraft's nose went down and it entered into a steep dive from which it failed to recover, primarily because there was insufficient height to do so. The biplane plunged towards the earth, hit a tree and then crashed into a stone wall, killing the pilot instantly and seriously injuring his passenger. In the opinion of the officer who saw the accident and who, as an airship pilot himself, possessed considerable knowledge of aviation, the crash was caused when 2nd Lt. Carter put his aircraft into too tight a turn in the gusty conditions prevailing at the time.

It was indeed possible that a gust of wind had caught the DH4 during its steep turn though it was equally possible, of course, that the machine could have been stalled by a tired pilot who made the mistake of relaxing his concentration too soon after a difficult flight. If this was the case, then it was a type of human error frequently found when a period of intense, stressful activity has been managed with some success and is almost at an end – but not quite. To the person involved it seems that the worst is over and he or she experiences a sense of relief and elation which is, more often than not, premature and even dangerous if the activity engaged in happens to be risky. In aviation it can be doubly dangerous because the trickiest part of any aerial journey – the landing – occurs at the end of the flight. But however the crash of this particular DH4 came about, it was the sad fate of the pilot to become the first aviator to lose his life as a result of a flying accident in Anglesey.

A touching, though slightly macabre view of the subsequent inquest is revealed in the *Holyhead Chronicle*'s account, from which we gather that 2nd Lt. Carter's body was placed either in or near the courtroom during the proceedings. 'At the inquest held on Friday', the *Chronicle* reported, ' . . . the jury returned a verdict of accidental death and expressed their sympathy with the [pilot's] father and relatives. Afterwards, the coroner and jury joined the procession accompanying the body from the court [at Llangefni] to the railway station as a mark of respect and sympathy.'

- 3 -

'Atlantic Flight Piffed!'

Though wiseacres scoffed when Lord Northcliff, the great press baron and aviation visionary, announced through the columns of his *Daily Mail* newspaper on 1 April 1913 that he was offering a prize of £10,000 for the first non-stop flight across the Atlantic, he was quite serious and sincere in his intentions, despite the 1 April date of the announcement.

While Northcliffe's idea was greeted by a chorus of dismissive voices as bordering on the lunatic and nothing more than a publicity stunt for the *Daily Mail*, critics were, however, wrong. The notion had a powerful potency which gripped the imagination of many a leading aviation pioneer – Gustav Hamel, for instance – but the outbreak of the First World War in 1914 caused all plans to be put into abeyance. Then, once peace was declared, the challenge was taken up again, following the resuscitation of the *Daily Mail* prize. Among the contenders were two RAF officers, Major Wood and Captain Wyllie and it is their story which concerns us here.

Unlike the rest of the field, all of whom intended to start from Newfoundland, to gain the maximum advantage from westerly winds, Wood and his companion, somewhat perversely, decided to make their attempt by flying from east to west *against* the prevailing winds, thereby making things doubly difficult for themselves. Why they chose to do this is not known but in the event it did not matter overmuch – they reached no closer to the New World than a few miles beyond Holyhead.

Our intrepid pair set off from Eastchurch, Kent, on 18 April 1919 in a modified Short Shirl, serial N111, a small single-engined biplane which Wood had named *Shamrock*, to fly to the predetermined starting point in Ireland; The Curragh, near

28

Kildare, hence the choice of an Irish name for the aircraft.

Modifications to *Shamrock* included a twenty-five percent increase in wing area and much greater fuel capacity – 435 gallons, giving a range of 3,200 miles cruising at 70 knots (80 mph). The extra petrol was stored in a huge elongated and torpedo-like container (the aircraft was originally designed as a torpedo carrier) slung underneath the fuselage. In this condition *Shamrock* was little more than a flying fuel tank.

The qualities of the Shirl as a type – stability, low fuel consumption and a high load carrying capacity – made it into an entrant in the transoceanic race in spite of the fact that the machine was single-engined, which was a disadvantage on such a hazardous flight as the one now being contemplated. Ominously, trouble had already been experienced with the fuel transfer system and leaking pipes during test flights but Wood, full of enthusiasm and dazzled by the glory that a successful crossing of the Atlantic would bring, took no notice of the warning signs. As reported in the *North Wales Chronicle*, Wood described the beginning of his journey thus;

> We started off at 3.15 p.m. on Friday, [accompanied on this stage of the flight by a 'shepherd' in the form of John Lankester Parker, Shorts' test pilot, flying another Shirl, [serial N112] taking a course north of London . . . our object was to make for Holyhead and use that point of departure for Dublin . . . Up till now the engine had been running perfectly and everything seemed favourable. We reached Holyhead at about 7.20 p.m. I then took over the control and Wyllie gave me the course and we started across the Channel. At the same time we commenced to climb as the clouds were rather low and we did not wish to lose sight of our pilot [Parker] and we got to about 3,000 feet.

Unfortunately, at this point – some twelve miles out to sea – technical problems put an end to the adventure. *Shamrock*'s engine stopped. Wood struggled to restart the now inert and silent power plant but to no avail. Abandoning his attempts, he turned the aircraft around and headed towards the Anglesey coast though he failed to reach land and eventually came down in the sea half a mile from the shore.

Two men belonging to a group of people enjoying a beach picnic at Holyhead saw the aircraft's involuntary descent and after a rapid search of the littoral in their immediate area the pair found a small boat which they, after encountering some difficulty in clearing water out of the craft, rowed to the rescue. But so small was the boat, it could only accomodate one other person and it so happened that Wood was rescued first. He was described as being 'very black' and was heard to mutter angrily as he got into the boat, 'Atlantic flight piffed!' Before land was reached, the tiny vessel became totally swamped and its three occupants were forced to walk through waist-deep water to shore. Captain Wyllie was rescued by the Holyhead lifeboat, which also towed *Shamrock*, floating upside down, into Holyhead harbour.

But what was happening, meantime, to Lankester Parker in the second Shirl? He, also, was in difficulties. Having followed *Shamrock* back towards land he then tried to come down in a field on the outskirts of Holyhead but though he alighted safely he could not stop the aircraft before it collided with a stone wall, and as reported in the *North Wales Chronicle*, his machine 'got badly smashed' in the collision. Luckily there was no injury to the pilot.

Both the damaged aircraft were eventually returned to Shorts, where an inspection of *Shamrock* revealed that an airlock in the fuel transfer system (whose faults, as we have already seen, were not properly cured) had caused the trouble. The second Shirl, N112, was rebuilt.

Major Wood, following his ill-prepared and unsuccessful flight earned the nickname of Atlantic Jim, which he could not shake off during the remainder of his RAF career. Although annoyed and deeply disappointed by the abrupt collapse of his ambitions even before the intended starting point of the oceanic crossing was reached, Wood was nevertheless lucky the flight had been 'piffed', as he put it, at the time that it was. Otherwise, if the same trouble had occurred far out over briny waters then the result might have been very different indeed. Most probably both men would have disappeared without trace into the ocean's cold, grey vastness.

As every aviation historian knows, the first non-stop crossing of the Atlantic (from west to east) was achieved by Captain John Alcock and Lt. Arthur Whitton Brown in a Vickers Vimy on 14-15 June 1919. After a flight lasting sixteen hours they landed at Clifden on the coast of Galway, Ireland. The landing area was boggy, however, and the Vimy's four-wheeled undercarriage dug in, causing a gentle upending of the biplane onto its nose in the soft soil. This slight mishap prevented the two flyers from continuing to London by air as they had planned and so they had to be content with a rail journey. First they travelled to Dublin, from where they crossed to Holyhead by mailboat on Tuesday, 17 June. At all stages of their journey – which had become a triumphal progress – they were acclaimed and lauded as heroes. Their reception upon arrival at Holyhead was reported thus by the *Caernarfon & Denbigh Herald* (20 June 1919):

Captain J. Alcock, DSO, RAF, and his navigator, Lieutenant A.W. Brown, RAF, winner of the *Daily Mail* £10,000 Transatlantic Flight, arrived at Holyhead from Kingstown by the morning mail boat RMS *Ulster* on Tuesday. The news that the intrepid airmen were expected by mail boat spread very quickly and by 11 o'clock there was a large crowd at the pierhead. Army and Naval Officers, Railway Officials, well-known public men were waiting anxiously for the arrival of the mail boat and this enthusiasm of the crowd knew no bounds.

When the vessel came alongside, cheer after cheer of real British welcome went up. The *Ulster*'s syren [sic] blew one great blast and the L & NWR Coy's ships followed suit. As the aviators – looking very fit and none the worse for their flight – walked up the gangway, they were again loudly cheered and many shook hands with them.

Mr Taylor, L & NWR Stationmaster, warmly congratulated the air heroes on their great daring and fine accomplishment and Alderman W.D. Jones also offered his congratulations, a vast crowd in the meantime surrounding the airmen. The visitors were escorted by Mr. Taylor to a special saloon.

In company with local journalists witnessing these scenes were their higher-ranking colleagues from the national press, including the *Times*, whose reporter wrote (on 18 June 1919):

Sirens, some booming a low note, some screaming a shrill one, chorused a greeting from the town and on the quay the fluttering of handkerchiefs of a throng of people could be seen. As soon as they got ashore – the crowd did not make this an easy matter – the airmen were met by Captain Vickers and Mr. Pierson, the designer of the Vickers Vimy – Rolls Royce machine [in contrast to the provincial *Caernarfon & Denbigh Herald*, there was no mention of stationmasters or local worthies by the vastly superior *Times*] and conducted to a reserved saloon on the London express.

The crowd, cheering and excited, surged after them and swarmed around the carriage. When Captain Alcock showed himself at an open window, a score of hands were thrust forward to get a grip of his fingers. Lt. Brown was also demanded and after he had acknowledged the call, ten minutes of furious autograph writing set in . . . .

Both men must have given thanks for relief when the whistle sounded and the train began to move. Five minutes later at Holyhead station the scene was repeated, however, with a still larger crowd and Captain Alcock's hand was nearly wrung off.

The run through Anglesey and along the coast of North

Wales gave a chance for luncheon to be taken and then came Chester with a civic welcome and a roar of cheers from as many people as could secure admission to the platform.

On Friday, 20 June the two aviators were the guests of honour at a lunch given in the Savoy Hotel, London, when a cheque for £10,000 was presented to the gallant pair. The man who presented the cheque was Winston Churchill, then the Secretary of State for War. In making the presentation, Churchill announced that he had received 'The King's gracious assent to an immediate award of the Knights Order of the British Empire' to both Alcock and Brown.

Thus, besides winning the *Daily Mail* £10,000 prize money the victorious airmen were also knighted by King George V, an honour which might conceivably have gone to Wood and Wyllie if only they had thoroughly tested the reliability of *Shamrock*'s fuel system. It has to be said, however, that even if the aircraft's fuel problems were remedied, the crossing of an ocean, especially in a single-engined machine, still presented a formidable challenge, given the North Atlantic's notoriously bad weather and the strong westerly winds that would have had such a retarding effect upon progress. In reality, Wood and Wyllie stood little chance of success. So formidable was the challenge of a non-stop crossing of the Atlantic from east to west that it was not achieved until April 1928, when two German pilots, Baron von Hünefeld and Hermann Köhl, accompanied by Commandant James Fitzmaurice of the Irish Air Corps, as navigator, flew from Baldonnell Aerodrome, near Dublin to Greenly Island off Labrador in a Junkers W 33 named *Bremen*.

4

Lockyer's Luck

In 1940, during the dark days of the Second World War, Daniel Lockyer, like thousands of other young men, was proud to be wearing RAF uniform, his pride further enhanced by the display of aircrew insignia on his tunic. He was, in fact, a wireless operator, of Aircraftsman rank, with No.240 Squadron of Coastal Command.

On Friday, 2 February of that year the Saro London flying boat (K6927) of whose crew he was a member was due to fly from the RAF's marine base at Sullom Voe, in the Shetlands, to the aircraft's home base of Calshot, near Southampton. The flying boat was heading south to receive a major overhaul, for which the facilities were not yet available at Sullom Voe at that early period of the war. Upon the outbreak of hostilities the RAF's flying boats were immediately deployed from their English bases to lochs in Scotland and the Northern Isles, to allow them to carry out patrols in the North Atlantic but it took much longer to build support establishments in the north, forcing aircraft such as K6927 to be flown to England for major servicing.

The two locations, Sullom Voe and Calshot, are as physically far apart as any two places can be in Britain – the distance between them being about 700 miles, but little did Lockyer realise when he settled into his seat aboard K6927 how long it would take him to complete the journey. He was one of eleven men occupying the aircraft that day: the pilot, Pilot Officer H. Porteous, co-pilot, Pilot Officer Smith, five crewmen and four passengers. These passengers were airmen going on leave from the windswept remoteness of the Shetlands.

To avoid possible attacks by enemy aircraft over the North Sea a westerly route was chosen, and the first stage of the flight, to Oban, on the west coast of Scotland, was achieved safely though conditions there were poor and rapidly getting worse. Indeed, the deterioration in the weather was so bad that the flying boat was forced to remain, moored – and marooned – at its landing place for some time, to the annoyance of the passengers, who seemed merely to have exchanged the isolation of Sullom Voe for nothing more than the tediousness of Oban caught in a bout of prolonged bad weather. Endless low cloud, mist and rain drove in from the Atlantic, obscuring the town and surrounding hills in a persistent grey fog of dampness and gloom which lasted throughout Friday and the whole of the weekend. If the reader will pardon a brief digression into personal reminiscence for a moment, the author can express some sympathy with the aircraft's crew, having once spent a June week in this particular Scottish location enduring the most dispiriting, oppressive weather imaginable – a continuous 'clag' of mist that reduced visibility to yards, and rain that varied from, at best, fine drizzle to, at worst, heavy downpours.

By Monday the crew had had enough of their stay and after K6927 was refuelled, it took off in what was, to begin with, fair visibility. Thus Oban was left behind as the flying boat's nose was pointed southwards on the next leg of the journey, a 160-mile flight to the Isle of Man. The cloud, however, soon thickened and reached almost down to sea level. Accurate navigation was now crucial in the bad weather but the navigator rose to the challenge and provided the pilot with bearings that took him to the island, whose highest mountain, Snaefell (2,035 feet – 621 metres) had claimed many a victim in conditions in which K6927 was now flying, though such an unpleasant ending was not in store for the aircraft. It would be allowed to fly on, at least for a little while yet.

Having reached the Isle of Man and at the same time successfully given its mountains a wide berth, the next step for the crew was to locate the small and easily identified islet known as the Calf of Man, just off the southern tip of the main island. This tiny piece of land provided a pinpoint from which to plot a bearing that would allow the Saro London to complete another stage of its flight, the pilot's intention being to fly to Anglesey, fifty-five miles away, with South Stack and its lighthouse, near Holyhead, providing a waypoint. Once the Anglesey coast had been located, the aircraft would then proceed towards its destination by following the Welsh coastline. But K6927 was now flying blind in the bad weather, prompting the pilot, Pilot Officer Porteous to change his plan. He decided to fly to a position some six miles off Holyhead while slowly descending to sea level with the intention of creeping in underneath the cloudbase towards Anglesey in order to obtain a 'visual' of the island's coastline. There was danger in this, of course. In the foggy conditions it was very difficult to tell where air and water met. To minimise the risk of flying into the sea, the method adopted was to throttle back and fly nose-up with a very gentle 'sink rate' or loss of height until the water was seen or perhaps heard as the aircraft's hull skimmed its surface.

Things, however, did not go to plan. A navigational error had been made, and the flying boat had drifted much closer to land than anticipated. Instead of arriving at a point a few miles off Holyhead, K6927 was heading directly for the port itself.

The first that Lockyer knew of the mistake was when he looked out of the window and saw 'a bloody great church spire going by on the port wingtip!' Pilot Officer Porteous saw the church spire also, and initiated emergency action. Lockyer describes what happened next.

The skipper lifted the nose and banged the throttles open to avoid any other unseen hazards. This resulted in a semi-stall and the aircraft struck water heavily. One wing broke free and the hull split asunder, rapidly filling with water. Everyone on board escaped, being either washed out, clambering free or being pulled out. Although on the London, the pilot's cockpit was enclosed, the three gun positions were open and the fractured hull offered a fourth escape route. We helped each other on to the remaining mainplane and, surprisingly, considering the amount of blood to be seen, there were no injuries apart from cuts and bruises.

Nothing could be seen through the fog and we had no idea where we were. In fact, we were inside Holyhead harbour. Shortly afterwards we heard shouting, and so we replied. A launch appeared out of the murk and picked us up. Wet through and very cold, we were taken ashore. There, we were most generously treated. An organisation for shipwrecked mariners fitted us up with a motley collection of clothing and we were taken to local hostelries to warm up. I was an aircraftsman at the time so I felt quite an impostor when fitted out with a tunic bearing three gold rings. Instant promotion! The rescue organisation also arranged for our oily, wet and salty flying clothing to be taken to the local laundry to be washed and dried.

Later, Lockyer was told that the flying boat had come even closer to disaster than he had first thought. It had flown so close to the masts of a ship at Holyhead that it had torn off the vessel's wireless aerial. If the aircraft had been only slightly lower it would have collided with the ship's superstructure, with a very different outcome to the accident, no doubt. Aircraftsman Lockyer and his colleagues were fortunate men that Monday.

On the following day attempts at salvage of the flying boat were made, with the aft part of the hull being towed to the beach at high water and the main hull dragged above the low water mark. This allowed the crew to recover items of clothing, suitcases and various personal belongings. The local laundry, in addition to dealing with the crew's flying clothing was also asked to help with the cleaning and drying of these other soggy, salt-water stained garments. It took two days. Then the crew were invited to the laundry to identify their own clothing and personal items. 'I arrived there', writes Lockyer, 'to find a bunch of giggling laundry girls peering at something on a table. Looking over their shoulders, I saw a small collection of what, in 1940, were very *risqué* photographs (although they probably would not rate a second look these days). I gather they were claimed by one of the two officers on board the flying boat.' During his unplanned stay at Holyhead, Lockyer was accommodated in a small hotel whose name he forgets but which was run by a Mrs Williams, a warm-hearted Welshwoman who was 'kindness personified'.

Lockyer did eventually arrive at his destination but only after a week had passed since he started out on his journey from the most northern part of Britain to its southern coast.

Early in 1941 he returned to Anglesey as a member of an aircrew whose job it was to ferry a Catalina flying boat from the Saunders-Roe base at Beaumaris to an operational Coastal Command squadron. During this visit, and subsequent others to Saunders-Roe he found himself attracted to 'a pretty lass', one of the company's many female employees. A relationship sprang up between the two and in 1943 Lockyer married his *amour*. After the wedding, both partners wondered – although neither told the other – about the possible length of their marriage. They were concerned, like so many other similar couples of the time, that the War and its cruelties might condemn their marriage to a premature end, blown out like a candle in the wind. Lockyer was well aware of the limited life expectancy of aircrew and as he had been flying since the start of hostilities, he felt that the dice were loaded against him and that his wife could be widowed at any moment.

But his luck held and he survived. He was clearly a man with good reserves of luck and a strong instinct for survival because he emerged unscathed from an operational flying career that included no less than *five* crashes. During his period of RAF service he was granted a commission, and eventually reached the rank of Squadron Leader. And if Daniel Lockyer was fortunate in his flying activities he was just as fortunate in his

38

choice of bride. What began as a romance conducted against a background of uncertainty about the future, engendered by the War, turned into an enduring relationship whose bonds are as strong now, in the serenity of old age, as they were when first formed by the fires and passions of youth, over half a century previously. Luck indeed.

5

Night Fighter Kill

The evening of Saturday, 1 November 1941 was a particularly good one for Pilot Officer Mervyn Shipard, an Australian pilot serving with 68 Squadron at RAF Valley – which, during that period of the war was a fighter station and was part of the defence cover provided by the RAF for Liverpool, Merseyside, and the North West in general. Shipard succeeded, much to his pleasure and satisfaction, in shooting down an enemy aircraft. But it was not such a satisfactory evening for a group of four *Luftwaffe* aircrew – they were the ones shot down. Following an interception, the Germans' Heinkel He 111 bomber was hit by cannon fire from Shipard's Beaufighter and crashed in the middle of Anglesey.

The interception was a typical example of the techniques used in night fighting; radar assistance both from a ground station and airborne equipment (the airborne equipment operated in this particular case by Shipard's colleague, Sergeant Douglas Oxby) to locate the intruder, accurate identification of the intruding aircraft to establish whether it was an enemy machine or not (with the intercepting pilot mindful of the serious consequences of a wrong identification!) then a careful stalking of the 'prey' before launching an attack. The outcome depended on whether the hunter had been seen by his quarry. If complete surprise was achieved by the pursuer then success often followed.

In these types of encounters there was a clear and deadly division between the victor and vanquished. The former lived to exult in his triumph, the latter went down, literally, to total defeat. There seemed to be a strong juxtaposition of luck – good and bad – in these conflicts, when one combatant's good fortune, almost by definition, brought the most extreme bad luck to the opponent. And in the savagery of war, bad luck more often than not trailed death in its wake – brutal, violent and terrifying. Such was the case of the four Germans, whose tragic fate it was that Saturday to meet their end on Welsh soil, at the hands of an Australian.

Shipard, in his combat report, written in the laconic, matter-of-fact style of all such reports, provides us with the details of what must have been an exciting night's work for him and Sergeant Oxby:

Valley take off 2024 hours to patrol Bardsey at 10,000 feet. Given vector 270°, EA [enemy aircraft] reported at 5,000 feet. I lost height to 7,000 feet and was then taken over by GCI [Ground Control Interception] Trewan Sands [located near RAF Valley]. RO [radio operator Sergeant Oxby] had contact with EA at 7,000 feet and maximum range then contact was lost but at 11,000 feet with further vectors from GCI contact was regained, EA 500 feet above and 30° to port, climbing . . . I made corrections bringing us within 4,000 feet range. I throttled back to 110 [knots] i.a.s. [indicated air speed] and 15° flaps. Closed to 2,000 feet then slowly to 1,000 feet and saw faint silhouette which I identified as a HE 111. I increased speed to 400 feet range then eased until dead astern 10 or 20 feet below EA. I opened fire at 300 feet with a 2-second burst – EA starboard engine caught fire and then the whole of the interior seemed to catch fire, the aircraft fell steeply to port, spiralling down until it disappeared in cloud at 7,000 feet. Our aircraft was lit up by an explosion beneath the cloud, later we saw the EA burning on the ground . . . After receiving more vectors with no results I landed at Valley at 2305 hours. During the action I had the moon behind me and apparently I was not seen by the EA as there was no evasive action and no return fire. I fired 62 cannon rounds. Weather 5/10 cloud, brilliant moonlight, excellent visibility. EA crashed six miles east of Valley.

signed; Pilot Officer Shipard

After the crash, the basic facts relating to the destroyed Heinkel and its crew were established: the aircraft, works number 0430 and coded F8+KR, was from the 7th Staffel of Kampfgeschwader 40 (the RAF equivalent being a Squadron and a Wing respectively) and was taking part in a raid on Liverpool. The bomber's crew members were: Leutnant Georg Leins (pilot), Unteroffizier Alwin Tepe, Unteroffizier Gerhard Fischer and Gefreiter Rudolf Terstegen.

Shipard's assessment of his victim's crash location as being six miles east of Valley was correct, the actual spot proving to be close to the farmhouse of Bwlch-y-fen Bentir and a nearby cottage known as Tan y Bwlch. These dwellings were one mile north of the village of Bodffordd. Occupying Bwlch-y-fen Bentir were David and Elin Jones, an elderly couple who became thoroughly alarmed upon hearing the loud noise of the flame-enveloped Heinkel as it dived out of control towards their farm. They hurried out of doors to investigate. Seconds later the bomber crashed with a mighty explosion which damaged the house and broke all its windows. If Mr and Mrs Jones had remained inside their home they would most probably have been injured by flying glass, shards of which had embedded themselves in the furniture.

The neighbouring cottage of Tan y Bwlch also suffered damage when two ceilings collapsed. Resident in the cottage was Thomas Ellis, his wife, their six-year old daughter, Nancy, and Mr Ellis's ageing father. That evening Mrs Ellis was doing some housework while her husband was working in a shed. Their daughter had spent the evening playing happily with a friend. Too happily, in fact, because when the little girl's bedtime came, she and her young companion were very reluctant to end their fun-filled play session and took no notice of Mrs Ellis's repeated entreaties to prepare for bed. Feeling exasperated at this recalcitrant behaviour, Mrs Ellis then called her husband, who said to the children, *'Cerwch i'r gwely, blant, mae Jerry o gwmpas heno'*, ('Go to bed, children, Jerry is around tonight') little realising how prophetic his words were.

Later, when the RAF and police came to inspect the wreckage of the destroyed aircraft – destroyed mostly by the detonation of its own bombs during the impact – the authorities were concerned about the possibility of unexploded bombs in the vicinity of the crash site and so the residents of Bwlch-y-fen Bentir were advised to leave their house temporarily, as were the Ellis family at Tan y Bwlch. All did so, with the exception of Mr Ellis senior, who stubbornly refused to listen to the pleadings, cajolings and threats of both his family and the authorities. The old man, regardless of any risk he faced from unexploded bombs, insisted on staying in his home – and he did! On the following day, he and the rest of the family had to contend with another hazard – hundreds of curious onlookers who came to view the downed Heinkel, or rather, what was left of it. Nothing would stop these people from trying to obtain a close view of the crash site and they cheekily trespassed on the Ellis's property, causing some damage and adding further upset to an already upsetting situation, especially for Mrs Ellis.

For her the crash was much worse than an upset. It was nothing short of a profoundly disturbing nightmare. To experience, more or less without warning, an extremely violent explosion and then to be confronted by the sight of badly mutilated human bodies, with severed limbs lying around, was deeply shocking for the Anglesey housewife, who was of a nervous disposition at the best of times. It was such a lasting trauma for her that even forty years later, in 1981, only with the greatest reluctance could she be persuaded to talk to the author about the events of that night.

Whilst the pilot's body was never found, the three other crewmen, Tepe, Fischer and Terstegen, were given a funeral with full military honours at Holyhead. Many years later, in the 1960s, their remains, like other German war dead buried in the UK, were exhumed and re-interred in the German Military Cemetery at Cannock Chase, Staffordshire. The date of their reinterment, in a common grave, was 5 March 1963. Tepe was only twenty-four when he died, as was Terstegen, whilst Fischer was considerably older at thirty-two but their leader, Georg Leins, was the youngest, at a mere twenty-one years old. He has no known grave.

6

Decoy Airfield Disaster

Throughout history, deception and bluff have always been a part of the tactics adopted by adversaries during times of war, and the RAF during the Second World War was no exception. It had a policy of protecting many of its airfields from possible enemy attack by constructing decoy airfields relatively close to the locations to be protected.

These decoys were of two types: those used during daylight hours and ones employed only at night. The latter were known as 'Q' sites and were fairly simple in design, consisting of nothing more than dummy runway lights set in open ground, and which could be switched on during darkness to lure any marauding enemy aircraft away from the real airfield. In Anglesey, RAF Valley was deemed sufficiently important to warrant the building of a decoy, the chosen site being Newborough Warren, an extensive area of coastal sand dunes in the south west corner of the island. Here, in 1941, a standard Drem runway lighting system was erected on poles fixed in the sand. The system was operated by a four-man team whose names are known: Corporal Barfield, LACs Jack Leaversuch, Thomas Baldwin and Leonard Morris. They were based in an enlarged Anderson air-raid shelter and each man worked a rota of three nights on duty followed by one night off. All four were billeted in the nearby village of Newborough.

For two years the 'Q' site sent out its false message into the night skies when requested to do so by Valley though not a single *Luftwaffe* raider was deceived into attacking the site, or Valley itself for that matter. In fact, only one aircraft was ever attracted to the decoy runway and that was during an attempted emergency landing, the consequences of which, quite obviously, were catastrophic. What an irony, therefore, that the aircraft in question was British. And more than that, what a tragic irony that this was all the 'Q' site ever achieved; to bring about an untimely end to the lives of two Allied airmen.

The accident occurred on the night of Thursday, 8 October 1942 when the Newborough Warren site was lit because Valley's resident night fighter unit, No.456 (RAAF) Squadron was engaged on interception exercises. This squadron had been formed at the Anglesey airfield in June 1941, with many serving Australian Air Force personnel among its members, and it was to be the only Australian night fighter squadron in the RAF. The unit operated Beaufighters.

Flying over Anglesey late that evening, whilst taking part in the interception exercise, was one of 456's machines: Beaufighter X8190 (a Mark VIF) piloted by a 20-year old Australian, Sergeant R. Scott, who in civilian life had been a shipping clerk in Melbourne. His colleague in the darkened confines of the aircraft was 21-year old Sergeant C.A.Wood, whose role was that of Observer/Radio Operator. He too was from Melbourne.

Extensive layers of cloud covered the island that night, though the Beaufighter, flying at 9,000 feet, was above most of this cloud. Everything had been normal until shortly before 11.00 p.m., when the machine's starboard engine failed. Scott reported this to Valley, saying that he was returning to base immediately. Following a descent through cloud strata the now-handicapped aircraft eventually emerged into clear air but, as if cruelly ordained by Fate, it did so over Newborough, where the dummy runway lights were burning brightly, radiating their spurious signals into the surrounding darkness.

Scott saw these lights, and no doubt under some stress, made the fatal error of assuming that he was at Valley. In doing so, he had fallen victim to the fundamental flaw contained within all 'Q' sites; they could easily be mistaken for real airfields by friendly aircraft. To prevent this happening, all the decoy lighting patterns had two safeguards: first, a screened bar of red lights across the dummy runway threshold, visible only from an angle of thirty degrees or less to the runway axis, and secondly, omission of the 'T' normally used to indicate where landing should take place. Scott, however, failed to note these departures from the usual lighting pattern and continued with his landing. Drawn like a moth to a flame, the Beaufighter quickly lost height and headed for the 'runway' – and disaster. During its final seconds, the doomed aircraft swept low, at a height of no more than forty or fifty feet, above the Anderson shelter, where one of the two airmen on duty, LAC Jack Leaversuch, was frantically trying to flash a warning with a small searchlight, but to no avail. Almost immediately afterwards, the Beaufighter hit the top of a sand dune, disentegrated and burst into flames. Within a few moments the 'Q' site duty crew were on the scene of the crash but such was the ferocity of the conflagration and so inadequate the rescuer's fire-fighting equipment – two pitifully small hand-held extinguishers – that tackling the blaze was a hopeless battle against overwhelming odds. There was no possibility whatsoever of rescuing the aircraft's crew. When the flames eventually died down, the pilot was found still sitting in an upright position in his seat within the wreckage while his colleague had been thrown clear but did not escape the flames. The two men were buried a few days later in Maeshyfryd Cemetery, Holyhead.

Very often in life, tragedy and comedy are close neighbours, and so it is with the story of Beaufighter X8190. Although the tale is a sombre one of loss and destruction it does have a lighthearted coda, whose details are well worth relating. Among the group who gathered at the crash scene during the clearing-up operation was a police constable whom we shall call P.C. X, a member of the Anglesey Constabulary and a man quite capable of bending the rules on occasions when it suited his purpose to do so – and the crash of the Beaufighter was one of those occasions.

When sifting through the debris, he found a wing tank lying some distance away from the main wreckage. The tank still had a quantity of fuel in it, so P.C. X, seeing an opportunity to get his hands on a few gallons of petrol, decided to steal the tank. He hid it in the soft sand and returned a few nights later, when all was quiet, to recover his booty, the contents of which, amounting to forty-five gallons, he shared with a friend. The policeman owned an Austin 7 motor car and could hardly wait to make use of his new-found source of fuel. He decided that he would take his wife to Llandudno, and so the car was filled with high-octane petrol despite advice from the constable's friend that this type of fuel might well damage the car's engine, though mixing a little oil with the fuel might, the friend said, help to reduce the risk. The advice went unheeded.

On the outward run, the little Austin's performance proved to be spectacular, much to the delight of its owner. 'It went like a bloody rocket!', he said to his friend. But things were very different during the return journey. There was a distinct haemorrhaging away of power, with quantities of blue smoke being emitted from the vehicle's exhaust. By the time P.C. X and his wife reached home, their car was incapable of anything better than a fifteen m.p.h. crawl in low gear. Upon inspection, the engine was found to have suffered burnt out valves and badly scored cylinder walls – perfect retribution for the policeman's misdeeds, some would say.

After the Beaufighter crash, the 'Q' site continued to operate until November 1943, when it was abandoned as no longer serving any useful purpose. By then the threat of attack from the *Luftwaffe* had diminished to such an extent that it could be disregarded altogether. The dummy runway lighting was removed but the Anderson shelter remained. In the early 1950s, when plans to convert Newborough Warren to an air-to-ground firing range for use by the RAF came to nothing* the land was

*In 1950 the Air Ministry proposed that Valley should become a base for an Operational Training Unit (No.61 OTU was put forward as a possible resident) under the control of Fighter Command and so a firing range was needed.

taken over by the Forestry Commission, who covered most of it with pine trees, though leaving the Anderson shelter relatively intact and little disturbed, a condition which endured for the next half century. Then, in 1992 the Commission decided to bury the shelter under tons of sand.

The burial was not total, however, as the Forestry Commission, in conjunction with the Countryside Council for Wales, had some laudable wildlife conservation in mind. Two small apertures were left in the sand-covered structure in order to allow convenient entry and exit for any passing bats that wished to make their home here. Placed alongside one of the apertures was the following notice;

'There are bats in this underground system. It is an offence under section 9(4) of the Wildlife and Countryside Act 1981, intentionally to disturb any bat using this place for shelter or protection. The penalty on conviction can be £2,000 per bat.'

So, dear reader, visit what remains of Newborough Warren's 'Q' site if you will, (map reference 413641) but disturb the bats at your peril!

Newborough Warren was surveyed and was under active consideration when, following a change in Air Ministry policy it was decided that Valley should go to Flying Training Command and consequently a firing range was not required. Thus was Newborough Warren, which has one of the finest beaches in North Wales, saved from becoming the sole preserve of the military. With the growth of tourism, the beach became one of the most popular in the region, and deservedly so. It is quite magnificent.

7

The Last Flight of Halifax BB275

At 3.15 p.m. on Monday, 1 February 1943, Pilot Officer
Cornelius took off in an Airspeed Oxford from RAF Tywyn,
near Aberdovey to carry out an army artillery cooperation
exercise. Shortly after becoming airborne and while still in the
circuit he noticed a Halifax bomber (serial number BB275) flying
at the same height as himself; 1,500 feet. The Halifax was from
1659 Heavy Conversion Unit based at RAF Leeming in North
Yorkshire. Aboard the aircraft was an eight-man crew, five of
whom were Canadians, including the pilot, navigator, flight
engineer and two air gunners. There was no danger of collision
between the Oxford and the Halifax, as the latter machine was
some distance away from the former and flying a much wider
circuit.

Cornelius noticed that only three of the bomber's four
propellers were working. The fourth, that of the port outer
engine was motionless, its lack of movement indicative of
engine failure, though it was clear from the fact that the
propeller blades occasionally made jerky, spasmodic rotations
that (unsuccessful) attempts to restart the engine were taking
place. The weather at the time, whilst not exactly bad, was not
good either; low clouds hanging over the nearby hills and
frequent, heavy showers of hail.

It occurred to Cornelius that the Halifax, which was engaged
on a cross-country navigation exercise (known in the jargon as a
navex) might be lost and the pilot was about to make a landing
at Tywyn, which, being only a small, grass airfield was entirely
unsuitable for use by such a large aircraft. Llanbedr, near
Harlech, twenty miles to the north and only ten minutes flying
time away, was a more sizeable airfield with runways and
therefore a better option for the bomber. Accordingly, Pilot

Officer Cornelius, hoping to save the Halifax from the consequences of a risky landing at Tywyn, flew his Oxford alongside the other aircraft, signalled to it by rocking his wings violently and began heading towards Llanbedr. But the bomber's pilot did not understand the Oxford's 'follow me' signal and remained where he was, leaving Cornelius to fly northwards on his own. When Cornelius saw that he was not being accompanied, he returned to the Halifax and once again waggled his wings. This time the other pilot got the message and began to trail the Oxford, keeping to port and one mile astern of the lead machine.

Everything went well until the pair were abreast of Barmouth. Flying at 1,000 feet over the sea, and two miles from the town, the machines encountered a particularly heavy shower of hail. Cornelius then switched his navigation lights rapidly on and off, indicating to the Halifax that he wanted it to keep up with him, which it did. Both aircraft entered the hail shower but only one – the Oxford – emerged from the other side. The Halifax had disappeared. As soon as the bomber was engulfed in hail it seems that the pilot took fright and pulled up in a climbing turn to starboard, abandoning the Oxford, whose pilot, continuing to flash his navigation lights, managed to catch a glimpse of the other aircraft as it gained altitude and headed inland into cloud. Its port outer engine was still not functioning.

The Halifax's somewhat aberrant and surprising behaviour, negating all of Cornelius's efforts must have been rather galling to him, especially as by then the runway at Llanbedr was in sight, even from within the hail shower. Now alone, the Oxford flew onwards to Llanbedr, where it circled the airfield a few times but Pilot Officer Cornelius could see no sign of his faithless companion and so, with his 'good shepherd' act a failure, though through no fault of his own, he landed and reported the incident to the authorities.

The scene now shifts in time and place to later that wintry afternoon and the Anglesey village of Four Mile Bridge, a small settlement located at the neck of the channel of water known as the Inland Sea, which separates Holy Island (and Holyhead) from Anglesey. Half a mile or so to the west of the village and adjacent to the minor road leading to Trearddur Bay, is the farm known as Old Turnpike. Working on the farm that day was twenty-year old Islwyn James, the farmer's son. Islwyn had been ploughing some fields, with a pair of horses providing the motive power and after the hard, physical effort involved both he and his animal charges were tired. The young man, however, was soon to forget his tiredness.

Shortly after 4.00 p.m., whilst stabling, feeding and watering the horses, James heard the deep, throbbing roar of an approaching aircraft's engines. Curious as to what the aircraft could be, the farmworker went out of the stable and saw a Halifax flying low from the direction of Holyhead and steering towards Valley. The machine was, of course, BB275.

Then the observer watched the bomber make a sudden, steep 180 degrees turn to the right until it was pointing in the opposite direction, before diving to the ground. The machine had, for some reason, stalled and spun in, impacting with fatal force in a muddy creek of the Inland Sea, only a short distance from the farmyard where Islwyn James was standing. A wall of mud was thrown up by the crash, shielding the death of the aircraft's eight crew members from the eyes of the farm worker. But he was quickly on the scene of the accident, having only a few small fields to traverse.

He found the bomber's nose buried deep in the mud and its back broken, though the tail section remained pointing upwards at an angle. James could see the dead body of the mid-upper air gunner draped across the fuselage. He had somehow been thrown out of the dorsal gun turret. Then the local doctor, a Dr Williams, arrived and proceeded to lift the farmworker bodily on to the bomber's fuselage so that he could crawl up to the tail turret to check the condition of its occupant, if indeed it had one. Upon reaching his objective, James could see it was occupied by a gunner. The man was quite obviously dead.

None of the people who came to the crash scene could gain entry to the aircraft but presently a group of RAF airmen arrived from Valley and proceeded to do just that, although they experienced great difficulty in removing the bodies from the nose of the Halifax because it was so deep in the ooze and mud. Not until 9.00 p.m. that evening was the last of the eight bodies brought out, in the fierce glare of searchlights, from the aircraft's wrecked interior. Islwyn James remained at the scene throughout and, in fact, assisted in the unpleasant task of carrying the bodies to the nearest road. As previously mentioned, five of the crew were Canadians and all were buried at Holyhead – two at Maeshyfryd Cemetery and the other three, including the pilot, at St. Mary's Roman Catholic Cemetery.

As for the Halifax, it was eventually cut up by the RAF and removed piecemeal from the site over a period of some weeks, during which time the wreckage became a magnetic attraction for local boys of all ages. Two questions remain: how and why did the bomber come to be in this part of Anglesey, and what caused the machine to stall? There is no clear answer to the first of these questions but it is obvious that the pilot after deciding, for reasons best known to himself, not to follow Pilot Officer Cornelius into Llanbedr, must have continued northwards, his actual path, and his intentions, unknown to us, until he came to the vicinity of Holyhead, either by chance or, more probably, deliberately so, hoping to land at nearby Valley and was approaching the airfield when his aircraft was first seen by Islwyn James.

With regard to the second question, an RAF Court of Inquiry revealed that the accident was due to engine failure and subsequent mishandling; that is, incorrect manipulation of the fuel system by the flight engineer after the initial failure of the Halifax's port outer engine. It seems, therefore, that when the bomber, which could fly relatively easily on three engines, was over Holyhead's Inland Sea, the aircraft experienced a sudden loss of power because of the mishandling of the fuel system, with the catastrophic and tragic results already described.

8

The Wrong Place . . . The Wrong Time

Through the malevolent caprices of chance, three people – Dr Mark Chill, his wife Marjorie, and her mother – became the unluckiest individuals in Anglesey on Monday, 19 July 1943. Without being in any way conscious of the fact, they happened to be in the wrong place at the wrong time and as a result became innocent victims of an aircraft crash.

On the 19th a Vickers Wellington bomber (serial number DV455), engaged on a training exercise, suffered failure of both engines whilst overflying northern Anglesey and so the bomber was abandoned by its crew, one of whom was killed when his parachute harness, which had not been fastened properly, became undone when he baled out. The aircraft slid earthwards, came down in a field near the village of Bodedern, tore through a hedge into a narrow lane along which a car was being driven, showering the vehicle with burning debris which set it alight and inflicted fatal burns on the occupants; Dr Chill, his attractive young wife and his mother-in-law. A million to one chance took their lives in a most appalling fashion. Seldom does bad luck manifest itself in such an extreme form as it did in this case.

Mark William Chill was, at the time he met his death, a 64-year old medical practitioner running a large, rural practice from his house in Bodedern. He shared his home with his wife, a strikingly beautiful woman less than half her husband's age. The other person in the doctor's household was his elderly mother-in-law.

On the morning of the accident, a surgery held in Bodedern occupied Dr Chill's time and in the afternoon his intention was to visit some patients in the nearby village of Llanddeusant before driving a few miles to another village, Llanrhyddlad, where he would hold his second surgery of the day. After lunch the medic said goodbye to his housekeeper and set off for Llanddeusant in his car, a dark blue Morris. He was accompanied, as he was more often than not, by his wife and mother-in-law. In fact, the Morris, with its trio of occupants, was a familiar sight on the highways and byways of this corner of Anglesey.

However, Chill had only travelled a few hundred yards that afternoon when he realised that he had left his medical bag behind. Stopping the car, he returned to his house, picked up the all-important item and then continued his journey, entirely unaware that this slight delay was adding another link to the chain of events conspiring to bring about an accident in which he would be involved. He was, of course, similarly unaware of the aerial drama being played out in the skies above him at that precise moment and how his own destiny was to become entwined in the outcome of that drama.

A few minutes after the brief inconvenience of the forgotten bag, the GP was driving northwards along Bodedern's lanes, heading in the direction of Llanddeusant. The weather was superb, with the sun shining out of an azure sky, bathing the countryside in a brilliant, penetrating light and giving three people (although they did not know it) their last view of the Anglesey landscape, bedecked, as it was, in its summer finery.

Shortly before 2.45 p.m. the good doctor drove past the church of Llanfugail, secluded and peaceful in the warm sunshine. A quarter of a mile further on lies the entrance to the farm of Tyddyn Watcyn and it was here that a hammer blow, as swift as it was savage, was delivered to the car and its occupants. One moment the Morris was motoring along, free and untramelled, without the slightest hint of danger presenting itself and then in the very next instant the vehicle was engulfed in a whirling, blinding maelstrom of flames, earth, stones, uprooted vegetation and flying wreckage. The crippled Wellington bomber had come down in a field adjacent to the lane, slid for a short distance along the ground until the aircraft collided with an earth bank on top of which grew a tall, thick hedgerow, smashed through this obstruction into the road beyond, where the hapless Dr Chill was unwittingly driving his car towards disaster.

His luck could not have been worse; a few seconds earlier and he would have had time to stop – a few seconds later and he would have driven past the point of impact. But a close shave was not to be. Instead, the doctor's Morris was caught directly in the cataclysm of violence – a cataclysm which turned this rural byway into a scene of tragedy. Burning fuel from the disintegrating Wellington drenched the car and set it alight with such speed that none of the occupants had time to escape. Chill, however, despite being seriously burned soon regained his wits and got out of the blazing vehicle. He would probably have survived if he had not then attempted to save his two passengers. First, he went to the aid of his wife and successfully managed to extricate her from the consuming flames. She was pushed into a roadside ditch by her husband, during which he himself received further burns but after this heroic effort Chill could do no more. Removing his elderly mother-in-law from the trap that was pitilessly incinerating her was beyond the medic's capacity. Abandoning any further rescue attempts he tottered weakly along the lane towards the farmhouse of Plas Llanfugail, adjacent to the church which he had passed but a short while previously, his world then secure and intact but now, only a few minutes later, it was in ruins.

A woman in the farmhouse heard the tremendous bang of the crash and was running towards the wreckage when she came upon Dr Chill with his clothes on fire. So badly burned was he that his facial features were more or less destroyed and so when the woman assisted him she had no idea that she was trying to help a man whom she knew well. She thought she was dealing with a stranger.

By now, others were arriving on the scene, including Ernest

Naish, a young naval officer enjoying a period of leave which he was spending at the family farm, located close to the crash site. Naish, like the helper before him, did not recognise Chill because of the severity of his burns but when the injured man spoke, the naval officer instantly identified the gravelly voice as that of his own doctor. This discovery shocked Naish but his military training helped him to remain calm and thus deal effectively with the crisis. Obedient to the GP's request that he went to investigate what had happened to Mrs Chill and her mother, Naish found that both were dead. The former had died in the roadside ditch where her husband placed her, while the latter remained inside the still blazing car, her body burnt and blackened. In reality, neither woman stood the remotest chance of surviving the accident, as ignited fuel from the Wellington had swamped the whole area.

Human flesh is often remarkably resilient and able to withstand some quite severe knocks but against the attack of flames it is defenceless. And in the ghastly circumstances the two females were in, the flames, fed by high octane aviation fuel, possessed a demonic, devouring ferocity which no living tissue could withstand. As for the Morris' driver, though terribly burned he remained alive and was taken in Ernest Naish's car to the hospital at Valley, where he died on the following day. Through cruel chance and bad luck – the worst bedfellows imaginable – three innocent people had perished.

* * *

Many years later, in the 1960s, Ernest Naish, after leaving the Navy, had returned to his first love – agriculture – and was managing a farm in Cwm Pennant, that most charming and beautiful of Snowdonia's valleys. One day in 1963 Naish was reading *The Times* and whilst glancing at the 'Personal' column he saw, to his surprise, that a woman who gave an Australian address, was requesting information on the whereabouts or the fate of a Dr Chill. Naish knew from his conversations with the doctor when he was alive that at one period in his life he practised medicine in the Far East and that he had relatives in Australia. Without further ado the farmer put pen to paper and wrote to the enquirer describing the events which had taken place in that Anglesey lane back in 1943. The reply Naish received from the Antipodes revealed the woman to be Dr Chill's sister, with whom the medic had lost contact. His sister wanted to know, for her peace of mind, if her brother was dead or not. The method she chose to make her enquiry had, in an amazing piece of good fortune, put her in touch with the *very* man who had helped her grievously injured relative twenty years earlier, thus proving, if nothing else, the efficacy of *The Times* 'Personal' column!

The sort of flying accident which took the lives of the Chill family is, thankfully, very rare and for any one individual the statistical probability of being killed by an aircraft dropping out of the sky is extremely remote indeed, and the Ministry of Defence has calculated that the chance of this happening is one in fifty-six million.* Yet, in 1972 Anglesey was to be the scene of a similar type of accident to the 1943 tragedy, the victim on this occasion being a middle aged woman in a caravan. The crash is described in Chapter 17. We will also meet Ernest Naish for the second time, in the story of Vampire VV659, which crashed near Valley in November 1954. An account of this incident is given in Chapter 11.

*As reported in *The Times,* 28 June 1980.

9

A Leap in the Dark

The log of HM Coastguard at Holyhead contains the following entry for Friday, 22 December 1944;

> 17.41 hours: Coastguard Peach reported having observed a vivid flash, similar explosion north of South Stack. Later confirmed aircraft crashed. Two men baled out and picked up, eight men previously baled out, whereabouts unknown. Extensive search combined military, police and Coastguards. Coastguards concerned: Rhoscolyn, Church Bay and Holyhead, Rhoscolyn and Church Bay Patrols, Holyhead Patrol, searchlight and lines [sic]. Nothing to report, (eight men missing).

In these brief notes, designed to convey the maximum amount of information using the minimum number of words, is outlined a wartime tragedy which, three days before Christmas – that special and traditional time for the celebration of human kinship – blighted forever the lives of eight American families.

The story begins on 19 December of that year, when a Flight of seven B-24 Liberator aircraft, including B-24 serial number 42-51232, named *the Jigs Up** belonging to the 36th Bomber Squadron, a Radar Countermeasures unit of the US 8th Air Force, set off from the Flight's base at Cheddington, near Tring in Buckinghamshire, on an operational mission which would take them to northern Europe. The seven aircraft, carrying secret electronic countermeasures equipment were, in fact, taking part in the Battle of the Ardennes. The Liberators' task was to jam the enemy's radar, thereby providing a measure of protection for American bombers participating in the (ultimately successfu)

*The name refers to a dance, as explained in *Webster's Dictionary* (Bookman's Press, New York, 1977), 'a lively dance, to dance; to bob up and down.'

campaign to halt what was to be the final German counter-offensive of the war in the West.

On the Flight's return to England, however, bad weather forced them to divert to RAF Manston, on the Kent coast, where all seven machines landed safely, thanks to the use of Fido.* They remained weatherbound at Manston until the 22nd, when, with a slight improvement in conditions the B-24s became airborne at 1.45 p.m. approximately with the intention of returning to Cheddington, only forty minutes flying time away. Each aircraft, according to the official accident report, 'had been "topped off" to 1,000 gallons of fuel' – an important point to which we will return later. At Cheddington conditions remained marginal and further diversions had to be considered, even as the aircraft were taking off from Manston. Accordingly, Cheddington's Flying Control section made arrangements for a possible diversion to Valley, which unfortunately was also experiencing bad weather: 7/10ths cloud at 1,200 feet and visibility down to one mile.

After the Liberators arrived at Cheddington, at 2.30 p.m. approximately, conditions there, as feared, were too marginal to attempt a landing and as it was not possible to return to Manston, the Flight was then diverted not to Valley but to the USAAF base at Atcham near Shrewsbury, arriving there at 4.00 p.m. Atcham, like the other airfields mentioned, was also in the grip of bad weather, though four of the seven aircraft did succeed in getting down through the low cloud and making safe landings. The remaining three were unable to do so as conditions had become too bad for them to take the risk. For the

*'Fog Investigation Dispersal Operation' but changed by the RAF to 'Fog, Intensive, Dispersal Of' in June 1945. Fido was a system which utilised heat to disperse fog from airfield runways. The heat was provided by petrol fed through pipes to burners sited alongside runways. It was an efficient system, used at a number of airfields during World War II, but had the disadvantage of consuming vast amounts of fuel. The aviation historian D.J. Smith states that, 'In round figures, Fido saved 2,500 aircraft and 10,000 aircrew at a cost of 30 million gallons of petrol.'

unlucky trio, it was a case of yet another diversion – this time to Valley, where, during the course of that short mid-winter afternoon (sunset was at 4.54 p.m.) the skies had become even more unfriendly: the cloudbase had fallen from 1,200 feet to 500 feet. Just before 5.00 p.m. the Anglesey airfield was informed that the three B-24s were *en route* to North Wales, with their Estimated Time of Arrival (ETA) at Valley being 5.30 p.m. The aircraft were *the Jigs Up*, previously mentioned, flown by Lt. Harold Boehm, *Miss-B-Haven* (serial number 42-50844), flown by Lt. Ralph Angstadt, and *Ramp Rooster* (serial number 42-50671) flown by Captain Richard Sackett. Lt. Boehm and his nine-man crew were not the regular occupiers of *the Jigs Up*, however. Their usual mount, B-24 42-50385, *Beast of Bourbon*, was unserviceable because of engine problems and so they had switched to another aircraft.

For *the Jigs Up* the cloud-ridden journey to Anglesey was not easy. Lt. Donald Burch, the co-pilot, explains why: 'On the way up we had lost an engine . . . and we lost our radar and radio . . . ' This included the loss of the all-important Gee navigational aid. Without this extremely useful, not to say essential aid, the navigator's task was made much more difficult. But, states Burch;

Our navigator [2nd Lt. W. Lehner] did a fantastic job [despite not feeling well]. He brought us in over [Valley]. He said fly two minutes in this direction and make a hundred and eighty degree turn and come around and you'll be right over the base, and . . . we were. He told us just by wind information that he had accumulated on the way up . . . , wind speed, direction, and all. We could see once in a while a break in the clouds and . . . I remember . . . seeing the base for just a few seconds.

Then we were in the soup again.

This was literally and metaphorically so. Not only was the aircraft flying in thick cloud but it was also rapidly running out of fuel. It had become something of a lame duck. Meanwhile Lt. Angstadt in *Miss-B-Haven* had full use of Gee. 'The Gee box got us to Valley', he said, though the trip was not without incident. The aircraft nearly came to grief in Snowdonia: 'The hills up there, some of them are high . . . we almost landed up on a hill [near Penmaenmawr] trying to keep contact with the ground . . . ' Upon arrival at Valley, Angstadt had the same problem as Boehm; a serious shortage of fuel. 'We were at the end of our gas tank', the pilot of *Miss-B-Haven* said.

As for the third B-24, *Ramp Rooster*, its pilot, Captain Richard Sackett, also had difficulties to contend with:

Well, the weather improved somewhat as we flew over . . . but as I remember, when we got there I know I was at six thousand feet between a couple of cloud layers . . . and we couldn't get any information as to how we could utilise the 'Buncher' beacon [a radio navigational aid] to remain in that area. So, we established a holding pattern [based] on the previous . . . winds that we had been given . . . some hours before.

This holding pattern could not be maintained for long. The Liberator's fuel supply, like that of its two sister-ships, was running out. One of *Ramp Rooster*'s air gunners, Sergeant John Houlick, said, 'We had about ten drops of fuel left.'

When the three aircraft arrived at their destination, a few minutes after 5.15 p.m., they discovered that they were not the only ones wishing to land. There were three others also: an RAF Wellington, a Douglas C-54 and a B-17 Fortress. The latter aircraft had a high-ranking officer, a Brigadier General, on board and had arrived from Prestwick after being diverted because of the bad weather. Thus, as darkness descended upon Valley, there were six aircraft present, all of whom shared the same immediate goal – to get down on the ground with the minimum of delay. First in this aerial queue was the Wellington, which landed at 5.27 p.m., followed by the B-17 at 5.34 p.m. In the meantime, the three Liberators, though all were short of fuel, had been kept waiting in a holding pattern. The question arises, did Valley's control tower know that the aircraft's fuel supply was on the point of exhaustion? Apparently not. The transcript of the tower's log for that evening records the initial exchanges that took place between Valley and the B-24s (*Miss-B-Haven* had the radio callsign 'Marker Item', *the Jigs Up* callsign 'Marker Jig' and *Ramp Rooster* callsign 'Marker Fox') as follows:

Time

1717	Marker Item	–	Ten miles east of field at 4,000 [feet], give landing instructions.
	Tower	–	Are you contact? Are you working high-frequency range?
	Marker Item	–	Roger.
	Tower	–	Hold position, remain above all clouds for further information.
1718	Marker Jig	–	We are behind Marker Item. We will follow him in.
	Tower	–	How is your gas supply?
	Marker Jig	–	Between *two and three hours* [author's italics].
	Tower	–	Roger. Standby.
	Marker Fox	–	I have *two hours* gas supply [author's italics].
	Tower	–	Marker Fox. What is your altitude?
	Marker Fox	–	6,000 feet, on top.
	Tower	–	Remain there.

If the aircraft were reporting plentiful reserves of fuel – two hours or more – then, as far as Valley was concerned, asking the pilots to 'hold' did not jeopardise the safety of their aircraft in any way. The controllers, in the light of the positive information given to them, could justify making such a request without any qualms whatsoever. In fact, such reserves of fuel, had they actually been in the Liberators' tanks, would have given a huge margin of safety. But we know, from the evidence already presented, that those reserves were not there. The tanks were rapidly drying up. If this was the case, how then do we reconcile the pilots' statements, as recorded in the control tower's log, with the reality of the situation which they faced? These statements are completely at variance with the facts. We will consider this point later, but for now, let us return to *the Jigs Up*, and the predicament in which its crew found themselves.

As the aircraft's last remaining gallons of fuel were being consumed, the tower was in contact with the pilot:

Time			
1722	Tower	–	Marker Jig, give me a call.
	. . .	–	[the Tower then makes other calls].
	Tower	–	Marker Jig, can you make an effective let down, how Radio Range?
	Marker Jig	–	You want us to let down.
	Tower	–	Standby.
1725	. . .	–	[the Tower calls the B-17 and informs its pilot he is clear to land].
	Tower	–	Marker Jig, hold your position. Will instruct you when to come in.

It was at this point that Boehm's problems boiled over into a serious crisis. Not only was he running out of fuel but his radio, once again, started to play up (both it and the radar equipment had been faulty during the journey to Anglesey, it will be remembered). This made it necessary for him to maintain contact with the tower by means of a relay provided by his colleague, Lt. Angstadt in *Miss-B-Haven*, also in the holding pattern, as was *Ramp Rooster*. Shortly after 5.30 p.m. Angstadt called the tower:

Time			
1732	Marker Item	–	Tower, Marker Jig would like an immediate let down. [Interestingly, the transcript does not contain an explanation as to why *the Jigs Up* wanted 'an immediate let down'].
	Tower	–	Negative.
	Marker Item	–	Can you tell me how many [aircraft] are down there?
	Marker Jig	–	Have no information about your [radio] range or anything, give info again, will you?
	Tower	–	(Gave Jig a long call).
	Tower	–	Marker Item, give message about Marker Jig.
	Marker Item	–	Marker Jig has lost an engine. [This message heralded the end of *the Jigs Up*].
	Tower	–	Roger. Will try to get him down as soon as possible.

At this time flares were being fired from the ground in order to try and help all the aircraft who were aloft keep in contact with the airfield. 'We could actually see the clouds lighted up [*sic*] where the flares were', said Lt. Angstadt. But this illumination was of little use to Angstadt's fellow-pilot, Lt. Boehm. For him and *the Jigs Up* it was too late. The situation had become irretrievable, though the tower did try to help, somewhat belatedly:

Time			
1735	Tower	–	Marker Jig. Standby, will try to get you instructions immediately.
	Tower	–	Marker Item. Can you pass information to Marker Jig?

1737	Marker Jig	–	No.2 and No.4 engines are unserviceable.
	Tower	–	Roger. Standby.
	Tower	–	Marker Jig, what is your altitude?

With the engines' supply of fuel having finally run out so did the B-24's time. There was nothing left except a glide through the dark, heavy clouds into the unseen world underneath, and then the inevitable, violent contact with the ground, the death blow that in an instant would turn a proud aircraft into nothing more than a million fragments of torn and twisted metal.The fact that the machine was without power meant that its captain was also without power to influence the course of events. His aircraft was going down and there was nothing, short of divine intervention (and the Almighty has always maintained the strictest neutrality in these cases!) that could be done about it. For the captain and his men, the only chance of survival was to abandon *the Jigs Up* without delay. There was no immediate reply to the tower's question, 'what is your altitude?' but two minutes later, at 5.39 p.m., came what was to be the final call from the aircraft: 'We are bailing out.' Don Burch, the co-pilot, stated:

' . . . the pilot gave the warning signal to get ready to bail out. I looked back in through the waist and the rest of the crew apparently didn't wait. They bailed out, I think, on the first signal, because everybody was gone when I looked back there.'

Listening on his radio to the exchanges between the crew of *the Jigs Up* was Sergeant Gordon Heath, *Ramp Rooster*'s radio operator: ' . . . one of the crew, probably one of the waist gunners in the back asked, "What are your orders, Sir? What should we do?" The guys said, "Bail out?" The pilot said, "Yes, bail out!" That was the last I heard of them on the radio.'

The Liberator's precise location at that moment cannot be ascertained though it is possible to deduce from subsequent events that the bomber must have been to the western, seaward side of the airfield, in the Rhoscolyn/Cymyran Bay area, and was flying northwards towards Holyhead. Once the eight crew members had gone, Don Burch exited the aircraft. He said of the experience:

> That was the one and only time I ever bailed out. I had a hard time going, but I went . . . I disappeared into the clouds and when that happened, I pulled the [parachute's ripcord] . . . As I broke through the clouds I could see the ocean over . . . on the one side of me, but I was over land – barely . . . I looked down at the ground . . . then I looked up and was looking around and the next thing I know [sic], I was on the ground . . . I just doubled up in a heap. Kind of sprang my ankle a bit. That's all there was to it . . . I landed in a farmer's field.

The field was at Porth Dafarch near Trearddur Bay and, in fact, Burch's descent had been seen by the field's owner, a Mr Morris, who went to the airman's aid. He helped Burch gather up his parachute and then took him to his home, where Morris' mother was preparing a meal. On the table was jam, bread and butter, spam and the Welsh speciality of *bara brith* (a type of currant bread, though more akin to a fruit-cake in its texture than bread). Don Burch was invited to partake of this simple repast, which he did with relish, making a sandwich out of the spam and *bara brith*, rather to Mrs Morris' astonishment and amusement, (*bara brith* is *never* eaten in sandwich form). While this was happening, Mrs Morris' son went to inform the authorities of the surprise American visitor sitting in his farmhouse.

Meanwhile, another local resident was also playing host to an unexpected American visitor. Lt. Boehm had come down north of Holyhead, on land belonging to Trefengam farm, on the outskirts of the town. Here, the farmer's wife, a Mrs Harper, looked after Boehm, preparing a hot drink and food for him and then informing the police of his presence. Once he had abandoned *the Jigs Up*, the aircraft was left to follow its final, unguided course – a course that could only have one possible end; a dive terminating in complete annihilation.

At 5.41 p.m. the previously mentioned Coastguard officer named Peach, on duty at Gogarth Bay immediately to the west of Holyhead mountain, saw a flash and heard the sound of an explosion in the vicinity of the North Stack cliffs nearby, which the officer then reported to his superiors and, as we have already seen, the information was duly recorded in the official log. What Coastguard Peach had observed was, of course, the destruction of *the Jigs Up*.

There was also a second witness, who was much closer to the scene of the crash. The witness in question was a Coastguard by the name of Harris and he was the officer in charge of the North Stack Gun Station, (the gun referred to being a fog warning device). Harris' report to his superiors reads:

At 1740 on the 22nd of December 1944 I saw a four-engined aeroplane heading in a dive direct for the gunner's dwelling from the East. When about a quarter of a mile away it canted its port wing up. It then headed West by North. Narrowly missing the dwellings and powder magazine, it crashed on the edge of the rocks at high water mark about 50 yards north of the gun shed and immediately burst into flames.

I took the fire extinguisher from my dwelling and leaving my wife to phone the authorities, I tried to subdue the flames, and while doing so there was a sudden burst of exploding ammunition. I jumped back and slipped on the oil splattered about and dropped the fire extinguisher in the wreckage. At 1922 I was informed . . . the crew of the plane had bailed out. The wreckage of the plane was smouldering at daylight [*sic*] on the next day.

> signed
> B. Harris
> Assistant Gunner

But the important question was what had become of the crew? Were they safe? As it turned out, the question could only be answered affirmatively in the case of the pilot and co-pilot. Sadly, the others had perished. When they baled out, the B-24 was over the sea and as none of the men wore a lifejacket, they had all drowned. Despite an intense and diligent search of local waters by the Coastguard, Holyhead lifeboat, and boats from the Royal Navy vessel, HMS *Bee*, the crew's bodies were not located, then or afterwards. A thorough scouring of the rocky coastline stretching from Rhoscolyn to Holyhead by policemen and soldiers from nearby units such as the 22nd Cheshire Regiment and 130 Coastal Battery also proved fruitless. The unregarding sea, having claimed its innocent victims, would keep them locked forever in the silent darkness of its watery depths.

In contrast, Boehm and Burch were, as we have seen, infinitely luckier. By the time they abandoned *the Jigs Up*, the aircraft, almost certainly flying northwards from Rhoscolyn, was over land and the fact that the pilot and co-pilot did not have lifejackets when they baled out was immaterial. In the case of Boehm, there was an irony in his survival. By obeying the code of conduct, derived from maritime tradition, dictating that the captain should be the last to leave a stricken aircraft, Boehm had, quite unwittingly of course, helped to save his own life. Thus, while his men died he lived.

Later that evening both he and Burch were taken to RAF Valley, there to await news – which did not come – of their colleagues. One can imagine how the enormous sense of relief and gratitude at personal survival would have slowly given way to feelings of great disappointment and regret as the hours passed and it became evident what had happened to the remainder of the crew. It is fitting, at this point, to record their names: 2nd Lt. William H. Lehner (navigator), Staff Sergeant Arthur R. Clemens (flight engineer), Staff Sergeant Frances J. Lynch (radio operator), Staff Sergeant Harvey N. Nystrom (radio operator), Staff Sergeant Jaime Fonseca (air gunner), Staff Sergeant Andrew Zapotocky (air gunner), Sergeant Roger F. Gagne (air gunner) and Sergeant Charles H. Dautel (air gunner). These men have no graves, having been lost at sea, but theirs are amongst the 5,126 names of missing US servicemen inscribed on tablets at the American Military Cemetery, Madingley, near Cambridge.

It is also, as regards the two men who survived, not unfair to point out that a dispute or disagreement of some kind occurred between them during the last few minutes they spent on the flight deck of their doomed aircraft. Indeed, the ill-feeling was strong enough to keep them permanently apart subsequent to the loss of *the Jigs Up*. At Valley, after the accident, they remained at a distance from each other and on the following day, when the other two B-24s, *Miss-B-Haven* and *Ramp Rooster*, returned to base, Boehm flew in the former aircraft and Burch in the latter. They did not serve together again in the Air Force and never met after returning to civilian life. The cause of this rift is still unknown. Boehm died in September 1991 without revealing the truth and Burch has chosen to remain silent on the subject, determined, it seems, to take the secret with him to the grave.

Returning to that December evening's events at Valley, events filled, as they were, with tension and anxiety, what, we may ask, had been happening to *Ramp Rooster* and *Miss-B-Haven*? While *the Jigs Up* had gone down to a disastrous end, the B-24's sister aircraft had managed to survive, though only by the skin of their teeth. Lt Angstadt of *Miss-B-Haven* tells his story, and in doing so, illuminates some of the problems faced by the Flight, one of those problems being, as noted already, difficulties in 'tuning in' to the local navigational aids – aids which would have made landing so much easier:

Valley did have the low frequency navigational aid but they wouldn't give us the frequency. So we couldn't orient ourselves . . . They wouldn't broadcast [the frequency] in the clear. No German aircraft had been over the place in a year or so, but nevertheless they wouldn't give us the information out in the clear . . .

However, if Valley did not want to divulge the radio frequency of their equipment, they were, as previously mentioned, more than willing to fire flares into the murk above the airfield. These flares were of some help to Lt. Angstadt:

We circled the flares, losing altitude. We were told that we could come on in and land as soon as we saw the field . . . As we broke out of the overcast we were headed [sic] in almost the exact opposite of the landing direction . . . We had to turn to the right a little bit in order to . . . make the one eighty [degree turn] back onto the field. We really made a very tight turn.

By this time, the Liberator's fuel situation was almost as critical as that of *the Jigs Up*: 'We knew,' said Angstadt, 'that we were sucking fumes.' 'There was no second shot at a landing. When we landed I don't think we had enough gas in the airplane to taxi.' The flight engineer, Sergeant Leo Hoffman, agreed: ' . . . we had just enough gas to get down and that was it . . . We didn't have enough fuel to light a match when we got down.'

All that mattered, of course, was that the crew members were safe, though perhaps their safety had been ensured more through luck than anything else. If *Miss-B-Haven* had remained in the air for much longer it too would have run out of fuel whilst airborne and there might well have been a double tragedy that night. Or even a triple tragedy if the third Liberator, *Ramp Rooster*, had not also experienced a little bit of the luck which had saved its companion. The *Rooster*'s fuel supply, like that of the others, was on the point of exhaustion after the time spent in the holding pattern at Valley. As air gunner Sergeant John Houlick said, 'We had about ten drops of fuel left.' He recollects those strain-filled minutes:

I remember [Captain Sackett] said there might be water down there. We had to strip off our parachutes and harnesses. This is a critical time! You're sweating now because you don't know whether to bail out or what and you haven't a chute on and the plane is starting to fall. So we took the chutes off and put our Mae West [lifejackets] on, then put the chutes back on; then I went over by the escape hatch . . . ready to bail out, whenever the word [was given] . . . I had my hand on the latch ready to open the door . . . Up front they would bail out through the bomb bay doors.

Then salvation came: 'We were cleared to land. [Captain Sackett] made one pass and made the landing and that was it. 'Sackett's feeling that 'there might be water down there' was, of course, perfectly correct and the decision to don lifejackets was, in the circumstances, a wise one, showing a degree of preparedness on the part of the captain for all the eventualities he and his crew might have to face.

Let us now turn to the official inquiry into the loss of *the Jigs Up*, which was carried out by what the USAAF termed an 'Accident Investigating Committee'. The investigation centred upon three questions: first, how much fuel the crashed B-24, and also its companions, had in their tanks upon arrival at Valley, secondly, was Lt. Boehm aware of his aircraft's fuel situation and thirdly, did those in the control tower know that all three Liberators were facing an impending crisis because of low fuel? There is little doubt that the aircraft were short of fuel but, as we shall see, this crucial fact is contradicted in some of the evidence.

On duty in the tower during the time of the crash was Technical Sergeant James Majeur. In his testimony to the Committee he said:

The tower's first contact (1717) was with "Marker Item" [*Miss-B-Haven*] who . . . asked if he could be let down through the overcast . . . I asked him if he was working

73

Henpeck Range and he said he was not. He was told to standby . . . until further notice. "Marker Jig" [*the Jigs Up*] reported in at 1718 . . . and . . . was told to standby. "Marker Fox" [*Ramp Rooster*] reported in shortly after and stated he was at 6,000 feet with about *two hours gas supply. "Item" reported he had about two to three hours fuel, as did "Jig"* [author's italics].

The reference made by Majeur to the healthy fuel-state of the three aircraft is puzzling to say the least and directly contradicts the strong evidence of the crews, evidence which has already been quoted. To make the point further, we can turn to the remarks of Sergeant Gordon Heath, the radio operator in *Ramp Rooster*:

I heard on the radio we were all getting low on gas. Everybody was concerned. You could hear the planes talking back and forth . . . I recall when we finally [landed], we had just enough gas to get down and we ran right up to the end of the runway. All of us got out and just kissed the ground that night.

The two claims – one suggesting there was plenty of fuel, the other that there was none – are quite obviously impossible to reconcile. Both cannot be correct but if we choose to accept Technical Sergeant Majeur's version, then by implication it reflects a degree of inefficiency amongst the three pilots, in that they had seriously misread their fuel gauges. It might be that *one* pilot on his own could have made this mistake but for all three, together with their co-pilots and flight engineers – a total of nine crewmen, all scanning the instrument panels of their respective aircraft – not to have noticed the worsening fuel situation is simply not believable. Incompetence of this kind amongst *three* different groups of aircrew approaching Valley would almost be beyond the bounds of possibility and very difficult to accept. On the other hand, the testimony of the crews themselves is much more credible and fits the facts.

We can glean something of the truth from Sergeant Gordon Heath. He speaks of the stay at RAF Manston and the subsequent refuelling of the B-24s:

At the time, the British were a little chintzy [chintzy = unfashionable, unenlightened, coarse or cheap, according to the *Dictionary of American Slang*, (Harrap & Co, London, 1976), but in this context Sergeant Heath probably means 'tight' or 'stingy'] on the amount of fuel they would give [possibly because of the large quantities of fuel used by the Fido system to land the aircraft]. I believe our plane would take 2,800 gallons to fill it up. In that case [the RAF] would only give us half a tank for each plane.

This ungenerous attitude was also noted by Captain Richard Sackett. 'We got what fuel we could from Manston but we couldn't get filled up.' As the accident report stated, the aircraft 'had been "topped off" to 1,000 gallons of fuel.' If the Liberators' tanks had been filled to capacity there would not, of course, have been any problems in maintaining a lengthy 'hold' at Valley. But with the fuel gauges barely reading 'half full' on take-off there was little or no margin of safety to speak of by the time Anglesey was reached. Little wonder, therefore, that the fuel situation of the three B-24s quickly became critical.

Besides Technical Sergeant Majeur, evidence was also given by his superior, Captain Quintus Feland, a Senior Flight Officer in the Flying Control Section at Valley. His report, like that of Majeur, refers to the Liberators' fuel position but contains two widely differing statements emanating, apparently, from one source – the aircraft:

At 1600 hours we were informed by the F.C.L.O. (Flying Control Liaison Officer) North West Filter Room that five of Cheddington's B-24s were over Atcham and would probably be coming to Valley. He was warned that our weather would probably clamp down after dark. At 1655 hours we were informed by Atcham that three of Cheddington's aircraft had been directed to us, ETA 1730 hours. At 1720 the F.C.L.O. passed plots on two of the B-24s (over Menai Straits) and stated that they had *ten minutes endurance* [author's italics].

The ten minutes of endurance reported to the FCLO is consistent with all the evidence of the crews and is indicative of the rapidly dwindling fuel supplies being experienced by the B-24s' pilots as they flew across Anglesey towards Valley. Yet, in the very next sentence of Quintus' report we read that, 'At 1725 hours the two aircraft were over the airfield, one at 4,000 feet, the other at 6,000 feet and both reported *two and a half hours endurance* [author's italics].' No explanation was forthcoming as to why the endurance had in such a short space of time been revised from ten minutes to two and a half hours. Neither was there an explanation as to why the Valley tower did not query or attempt to clarify the widely differing fuel-state reports which had been received. This was not a minor point of little consequence – on the contrary, endurance and fuel supply was a matter of the utmost seriousness with regard to the safety of the aircraft.

Captain Feland ended his report with a reference to the rescue attempt that was organised after the crash of *the Jigs Up*:

At 1745 [hours] the Coastguard at South Stack reported having seen an aircraft crash into the sea off South Stack. Air/Sea Rescue action was taken immediately. By 1915 hours two of the crew had been found . . . By 2330 hours, information received from the pilot made it appear probable that the other members of the crew (8) had bailed out over the sea. Search parties were recalled, "the search abandoned until daylight."

After deliberating over this and the other reports, the Investigating Committee came to its conclusions, and aimed a trident of criticism at those whom it deemed to be responsible for causing the loss of the Liberator. Impaled upon the trident's prongs were Cheddington's Flying Control section, the pilot of the aircraft and those whose job it was to brief the crew. The Committee made the following comments:

First, Flying Control; the flight should have been diverted to Valley immediately after it had become evident that they could not land at Cheddington. Much valuable time had been lost by sending the flight to Atcham, whose weather at the time was uncertain.

Then the hapless Lt. Boehm:

Second: the pilot should have kept a more accurate check on his fuel supply. At the time the engines were failing, the pilot did not realize that he was getting short of fuel, however, during the investigation he readily conceded that this was the only plausible reason for the engine failures.

And thirdly:

The crew had not been properly briefed on terrain and airport facilities in the area. The pilot had no knowledge whatsoever of the radio range at Valley nor did he know the position of the mountains in relation to the airdrome [sic]. At the time the pilot gave the order to bail out he did not know that the airport was situated on an island and the probability of his fellow crew members landing in the sea [sic]. They were depending entirely on [the] "G" box for navigation and when this went out they had no means of making an exact check on their position.

But the question has to be asked, did the Committee treat all the parties concerned in an even-handed manner when it came to apportioning blame? Was the judgement fair and objective in its criticism? Only partly so. If we take into consideration the inconsistencies contained within the various accounts and examine what the reasons for those inconsistencies might be, then in the light of that examination blame has to be redistributed amongst those held to be responsible for causing the accident.

Certainly, the condemnation of the decision not to divert the aircraft to Valley immediately after they were prevented from landing at Cheddington seems reasonable. If this had happened, then in all probability *the Jigs Up* would have been saved. As the Committee pointed out, 'much valuable time had been lost by sending the flight to Atcham . . . '

The criticism of the lack of a proper briefing for the crews is also justified. Their unawareness of Valley's facilities and especially of the local topography was one of the main contributory causes of the disaster. Even knowledge of one simple fact, that of Valley's location – on the coast of an island – would have ensured the wearing of lifejackets by the crew of *the Jigs Up* as they baled out into the winter gloom. There would have been every likelyhood also of a liferaft being deployed, thus vastly improving their chances of survival. Tragically, they were in the dark in more ways than one.

In the case of Lt. Boehm, however, the Committee's reproachful attitude seems a little harsh. His was not the only aircraft running out of fuel – all three B-24s were in this position. The evidence of crew members in *Ramp Rooster* and *Miss-B-Haven* is strong and consistent on this important point. As we have seen, there was considerable discussion taking place between the crews on the worsening fuel situation. If Boehm had been on his own then perhaps the criticism of his alleged failure to 'realise that he was getting short of fuel' and that he should have 'kept a more accurate check on his fuel supply' might have some validity. But, as already noted, the co-pilot and flight engineer would also have been monitoring the aircraft's instruments, including the fuel gauges. If those gauges were indicating a serious lack of fuel then the pilot's colleagues would surely have alerted him to this fact, even if he himself had failed to notice it.

We also have to judge the accuracy or otherwise of the control tower log transcript. If we assume the transcript to be a

78

true record, then the radio call made by Boehm, timed at 1718 hours, stating that he had 'between two and three hours' of fuel, lets Valley off the hook as far as their treatment of him is concerned. With that amount of unused fuel in his aircraft's tanks he could spend a lengthy period, if necessary, waiting in the holding pattern without any risk of compromising safety. There was no hurry to get him on the ground. But at the same time as it showed Valley to have behaved correctly, the radio call casts a shadow on Boehm. How was it that he reported enough fuel to last 'between two and three hours' and yet only twenty minutes later he and his crew abandoned their aircraft because its engines were failing due to lack of fuel? Could his monitoring of the fuel gauges have been that inept? Yes, according to the Investigating Committee, who accused him of not realizing 'that he was getting short of fuel' and then drew from him the admission 'that this was the only plausible reason for the engine failures.'

Consider, however, the combined testimony of the other two aircraft's crews – testimony which points to the one factor that was of overriding concern to them; they were all running short of fuel. The weight of that evidence relieves Boehm somewhat of the charge of inefficiency. It seems unfair to single him out as being guilty of shortcomings when, in fact, all three pilots were in exactly the same position. What can be said of Lt. Boehm is that he was unlucky rather than blameworthy, because his was the only one of the three B-24s which actually ran out of fuel before it could land. While the other two aircraft came within a hairsbreadth of being caught in the same noose, it was their pilots' good fortune to have sufficient fuel – just – and Boehm's misfortune not to.

We also have to consider the possibility that Valley might have been aware of the Liberators' fuel shortages but for some reason chose to ignore this and did not give the aircraft the landing priority which they required. If this was true, then there had to be an explanation for the decision to put them in a holding pattern. For the B-24s' crews that reason was not hard to discern. Staff Sergeant Harry Setzer, *Miss-B-Haven*'s radio operator said;

'I remember . . . a general in the [landing] pattern, coming in and he had priority. [His aircraft] had the [radio-range] frequency, we didn't. We were having trouble getting communication with the tower at that time. They kept telling us to hold and circle the flare . . . They said we had one other plane in the pattern [the general's] and he was to land. That was it.

Sergeant John Houlick of *Ramp Rooster*, in echoing this view, must surely have come close to the truth:

We had to wait because a general was coming in, and we were all low on fuel. They held us up to let that general land. The general landed and then we got permission to come in. That's why we held in that pattern for a little while.

If we look at this highly plausible explanation for Valley's tardiness in allowing the Liberators to land, Boehm's guilt is further diminished. Looked upon in this light he is seen not as a pilot who committed an error but as a luckless victim, made into a scapegoat by the authorities when there were others at Valley equally, if not more, deserving of censure because they broke air traffic control rules. Whilst generals ordinarily have precedence over lower ranks, nevertheless an emergency in the air should always have priority over other traffic, whether that traffic includes a high-ranking officer's aircraft or not. Emergencies come first.

Interestingly enough, another aspect of this affair is revealed by a confidential document, 'Problems of Co-ordinating with British Organizations', written at that time. The document, now contained within the historical record of the American unit at Valley (the 1407th AAF Unit, Air Transport Command) discussed the difficulties sometimes faced by the Americans in

*Robert Loraine (seated) looks on while his mechanic, Jules Vedrines,
carries out adjustments to the biplane.
In the background is Loraine's friend, George Smart.*
Photo: Crown copyright

Loraine's biplane at Rhos-on-Sea, 10 August 1910.
Photo: Gwynedd Archives

The wreckage of DH4 A7654, whose crash at Llangefni in November 1917 was Anglesey's first fatal air accident.
Photo: Crown copyright

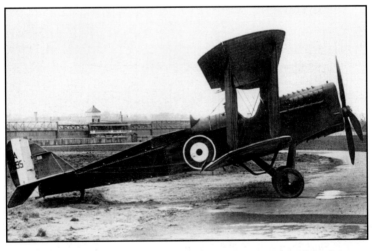

An Airco DH4 *similar to the one that crashed at RNAS Llangefni.*
Photo: Map

Short Shirl **Shamrock** *about to set off on an attempt at crossing the Atlantic in April 1919. Note the massive extra fuel tank slung underneath the fuselage.*

Photo: Caernarfon Air Museum

Short Shirl **Shamrock** *in Holyhead harbour after the failed attempt on the Atlantic crossing.*

Photo: Daily Mirror

*Daniel Lockyer during the early
days of his RAF career.*

Photo: Squadron Leader D. Lockyer

*Rear fuselage section of wrecked Saro
London K6927 beached at Holyhead.*

Photo: via Squadron Leader D. Lockyer

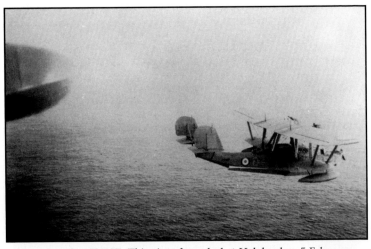

Saro London K6927. *This aircraft crashed at Holyhead on 5 February,
1940.*

Photo: via Squadron Leader D. Lockyer

The Bodffordd field into which Heinkel F8+KR *crashed,*
November 1941.
Photo: David Roberts

A Heinkel HE111 *bomber similar to the one that was shot down near*
Bodffordd on 1 November 1941.
Photo: Map

A Bristol Beaufighter similar to the one that crashed at the Newborough Warren 'Q' site on 8 October 1942.

Photo: Map

The remains of the Newborough Warren 'Q' site, photographed in 1981.

Photo: Roy Sloan

R. Islwyn James, who was first on the scene of the crash of Halifax BB275, *photographed at the crash site in 1997.*

Photo: Roy Sloan

A Handley Page Halifax bomber similar to the one that crashed at Four-Mile Bridge on 1 February 1943.

Photo: Map

*The lane where Dr Chill and his family met their deaths. The collision
between* **Wellington DV455** *and Dr Chill's car took place at the point where
the tree's shadow is located.*
Photo: Roy Sloan

*A Vickers Wellington bomber similar to the one that crashed near Bodedern
on 19 July 1943, fatally injuring Dr Mark Chill and his family.*
Photo: Map

The Jigs Up *nose art.*
Photo: Dr Robert F. Hambaugh Jr.

B-24 Liberator 42-51232 Jigs Up *which ran out of fuel whilst attempting to land at RAF Valley on 22 December 1944.*
The aircraft crashed near North Stack, Holyhead.
Photo: Roy W. Stroud

B-24 Liberator 42-50844 Miss-B-Haven, *sister-ship to* Jigs Up.
Though in a similarly fuel-starved state as its companion, Miss-B-Haven
succeeded in landing at Valley on 22 December 1944.
Photo: Jack W. Charlton

B-24 Liberator 42-50671 Ramp Rooster, *the third of the trio of fuel-starved*
B-24s. Like Miss-B-Haven, *this aircraft managed to land safely at Valley.*
Photo: Don C. Albinson

Memorial to the crew of Jigs Up,
Breakwater Quarry Country Park, Holyhead.
Photo: Roy Sloan

The cockpit of B-24 Liberator Jigs Up.
Photo: Melvin A. Remus

The crew of Jigs Up. *From left to right: Sgt Charles Dautel, Staff Sgt Jaime Fonseca, Staffs Sgt. Arthur Clemens, Staff Sgt Roger Gagne (kneeling), Staff Sgt Harvey Nystrom (standing), 2nd Lt William Lehner, 1st Lt. Harold Boehm, 2nd Lt. Donald Burch, Staff Sgt Andrew Zapotocky. The tenth member of the crew, Staff Sgt Frances Lynch, is not in the photograph.*
Photo: Jack W. Charlton

The crash of Spitfire L1034 at Beaumaris on 13 March 1941.
Photo: via Olwen Williams

de Havilland Vampire FB5 WA332 at RAF Valley in 1951. This aircraft is similar to the one successfully ditched by Pilot Officer Peter Dimmock in July 1951. It is similar also to the many other single-seat Vampires that came to grief at Valley during the 1950s.

Photo: Geoffrey Siers

A group of student pilots from 202 AFS, RAF Valley, in 1951. Standing on the right is a Persian officer, Captain Sirang, who lost his life in the crash of Vampire FB5 WA298 on 2 July 1951.

Photo: via Geoffrey Siers

The crash of Vampire XD620 at Rhostrehwfa on 8 August 1962.
Photo: via Arthur Evans

An example of a two-seater Vampire, the T.11, which served as an advanced trainer at RAF Valley during the 1950s and early 1960s. A number of these aircraft were lost in flying accidents in Anglesey.
Photo: via Arthur Evans

*Impact point of Sea Fury F-25 of the Dutch navy after the mid-air collision
with Sea Furies F-43 and F-28 near Rhydwyn, 19 May 1953.*
Photo: Crown copyright

*Wreckage of Sea Fury F-25 lies near the farmhouse of Pen-y-Foel, Rhydwyn.
Damage to the building's roof can be clearly seen.*
Photo: Crown copyright

The tailplane and rear fuselage of Sea Fury *F-25.*
Photo: Crown copyright

Wreckage of Sea Fury *F-25 lying in one of Pen-y-Foel's fields.*
Photo: Crown copyright

dealing with their RAF colleagues and notes 'a particularly delicate situation' in Valley's control tower. It will be remembered that the airfield, from 1943 onwards, became an important trans-Atlantic staging post for American bombers, a role which left the RAF in a somewhat subordinate position to the USAAF unit. This resulted in low morale, as bemoaned by the Station Commander during the summer of 1944. 'Morale would improve', he wrote, 'if British aircraft could either be stationed at Valley . . . or if larger numbers of RAF aircraft could be directed from overseas . . . the lack of RAF traffic is generally disappointing.' That is how it remained, however, and American dominance continued. The first appearance of Americans in the control tower seems to have caused some friction, as evidenced by the document already referred to.

> During the month of December [1944] a particularly delicate situation arose in respect to the controlling authority and responsibility within the Control Tower. Up until this time British personnel alone staffed the control offices and naturally the assignment of AAF Control officers brought the subject of final authority to focus. Discussions of policy and skills resulted in the publication of a directive . . . by the Officer Commanding, R.A.F. Station Valley, as a temporary settlement of the problem. Interviews with the Flying Control Officer indicates that further co-ordination will be necessary to establish joint control in the true sense of the phrase.

Whilst these disharmonies might not have contributed directly to the loss of *the Jigs Up*, they certainly did little to promote efficiency amongst the air traffic controllers. Although relationships might have been strained within the control tower, the American unit's commander, Colonel James C Cochran, wasted no time in expressing his thanks to the British helpers in the fruitless search for the crew of the crashed Liberator. On the day after the accident, he wrote as follows:

Gentlemen,

The Commanding Officer, Officers, and men of the 1407th AAF Base Unit desire to express, on behalf of themselves and the United States Army Air Forces, thanks for your immediate and generous help in the attempt to locate and aid missing U.S.A.A.F. airmen on the night of 22 December 1944.

We feel that this constitutes one of the most concrete examples of practical Anglo-American solidarity that we have seen, and wish to let it be known that we are very thankful for the courtesy and consideration which you have shown.

Signed,
James C. Cochran
Colonel, Air Corps,
Commanding.

Recipients of this letter were the Royal Observers Corps, Caernarfon, 22nd Cheshire Regiment, Trearddur Bay, 130th Coastal Battery, Llanfwrog, 307th Holding Battalion, Rhosneigr, Royal Artillery AA Practice Camp, Tŷ Croes, personnel of HMS *Bee*, Holyhead, and RAFs Valley, Bodorgan, Mona, and Llandwrog.

As regards the effect of the crash upon Lt. Boehm, one of the 36th Bomb Squadron's air gunners, Technical Sergeant Henry 'Hank' Parke, provides this view of the man's tumbling self-confidence and doubts about his future as a pilot – doubts which were soon dispelled by the entreaties of Parke and others:

Boehm took [the accident] awful hard, and there was nothing he could do about it. . . . He felt responsible for losing [the crew]. Boehm didn't want to fly any more. Me and one other fellow, Fred Neiser, went to see him. We didn't have a crew and wanted to get going. We talked him into taking us. We got him a whole crew and he flew again. I flew tail gunner for him . . . When he took us on as a crew . . . he said, "There's only one thing I'm gonna tell you guys . . . You're gonna wear your Mae West. If I ever catch anybody without their Mae West on in that plane you're done flying with me." He wasn't going to have [what happened in *the Jigs Up*] happen again. I can't blame him for that.

But whatever the depth of Boehm's regrets and whatever the arguments over the fairness or otherwise of the official investigation, nothing could alter the fact that eight men had lost their lives in tragic circumstances. When those unfortunate Americans parachuted out of their aircraft, they would have expected to feel the reassurance of solid earth upon landing. How terrible, therefore, the shock must have been for them when they found themselves plunging into ice-cold water. Instead of reaching safety, the men had merely exchanged the entrapment of their doomed aircraft for the equally fatal entrapment of the sea. A leap into the darkness of a December night became a leap into eternal darkness.

* * *

Some flying accidents in Anglesey and Gwynedd have sequels (see Chapter 12)* and the loss of *the Jigs Up* is amongst them. In May 1992 an American named Stephen Hutton from Apex, North Carolina, came to Holyhead to enquire about the Liberator's crash, as the enquirer's father, Iredell Hutton, had been the rear gunner of the aircraft, though luckily not on its last flight, (the B-24 was not being flown by its regular crew on that occasion, it will be remembered). Stephen Hutton was directed to the Coastguard office, where he was given all the information that was available. Subsequently the American, an air traffic control specialist by profession, went on to research not only the crash of the Liberator in great detail but also the history of the

*See also the author's *Aircraft Crashes – Flying Accidents in Gwynedd 1910-1990*, (Chapters 5 and 7) and Edward Doylerush's *No Landing Place*, vol I (Chapter 6) and vol II (Chapter 1).

squadron to which the aircraft belonged. This research culminated in the publication of a book, *Squadron of Deception* (see Bibliography) containing a very full account of the events leading to the loss of *the Jigs Up* and upon which the present narrative is based.

A month after Hutton's visit to Holyhead a group of local divers, Brendan Maguire, Graham Wright and John McGuigan, began to explore the underwater crash site at North Stack. On 17 June, Maguire located the wreckage, including a propeller blade, which was recovered by him. A week later, on 24 June, Maguire found, and recovered, a second blade.

It was then decided that one blade would form the centrepiece of a memorial plaque to be erected in the newly-created Breakwater Quarry Country Park near North Stack while the second blade was to be taken to the United States, where it would find a fitting home in a military museum. Thus, on Sunday, 18 April 1993, in unpleasant conditions of driving rain an open-air service and unveiling ceremony took place at Holyhead. Among those attending were Brendan Maguire, Graham Wright and John McGuigan plus Stephen Hutton, his wife, and his parents. It was 73-year old Mr Hutton senior, watched by Coastguards, Service personnel and a crowd of spectators, who performed the actual duty of unveiling the plaque. A trumpeter sounding the Last Post provided an emotional climax as the Stars and Stripes, Red Dragon, Royal British Legion and other flags were lowered. Then a Wessex SAR helicopter from RAF Valley, trailing the RAF Ensign, flew over the site of the memorial.

It had been hoped that Harold Boehm would carry out the unveiling duty but he had died in 1991 and so his former colleague, Don Burch, was approached instead and an invitation to visit Anglesey was extended to the ex-pilot. Burch, however, declined the invitation. He felt that such a visit and all that it entailed would prove much too distressing for him.

On 12 March 1994, eleven months after the Holyhead

ceremony, the second of the two propeller blades was unveiled at a similar event held 3,500 miles away at Fort Fisher Military Museum, North Carolina. Present was Stephen Hutton, together with his wife Pamela and his father, Iredell. Present also were relatives of the eight men who had lost their lives. Another leading figure at the gathering was Brendan Maguire, who was accompanied by his wife and children. For Maguire this was an important day. He felt strongly that the eight drowned aircrew should not be forgotten and he had been instrumental in setting up both the Holyhead and Fort Fisher remembrances. Thus with memorial plaques in place on both sides of the Atlantic, he and like-minded friends such as Stephen Hutton could feel well-satisfied with their efforts to honour those lost in the tragedy of *the Jigs Up*.

10

A Miscellany of Second World War Accidents

Although the Second World War saw many serious and tragic flying accidents on Anglesey soil, it is true that for every major crash there were half a dozen or more who cannot be described as disastrous or catastrophic in the sense that there was loss of life or grievous injury inflicted upon victims. For every pilot killed, plenty escaped from the wrecks of broken aircraft with nothing worse than cuts and bruises, and perhaps a dented ego. In other words, some men were lucky, others were not, as in life generally. This chapter describes, in a condensed manner, twenty accidents and in doing so attempts to give the reader a brief, snapshot view of incidents ranging in their effect from the trivial to the fatal.

Bristol Blenheim L1185, Bodorgan, 4 March 1940

This aircraft belonged to 104 Squadron and was based at RAF Bicester, in Oxfordshire. At 10.00 a.m. on the day of the crash L1185 took off on a cross country navigation exercise (known as a 'navex') which would take it to Jurby in the Isle of Man, then to Scotland and finally back to base. The weather at Bicester was reasonable at the time of the take-off but over North Wales there was low cloud and the Blenheim quickly went off track when it entered this cloud. Once visual references with the ground were lost the crew's DR (Dead Reckoning) navigation techniques failed them. The pilot elected to make a descent through cloud (always a risky procedure if an aircraft's position is uncertain) and when the bottom of the cloudbase was reached the three-man crew found themselves flying over the sea – the Irish Sea, in fact – and at such a low altitude that, according to the Air

Gunner, spray from the waves was hitting the aircraft.

Be that as it may, the pilot said he would head for the airfield of RAF Squires Gate, on the outskirts of Blackpool. The Air Gunner, however, had a strong feeling in his bones that Squires Gate would not be seen that day. He was right. No sooner had the pilot made his decision than his mind was very rapidly and forcibly changed for him when, all of a sudden, out of the marine mist and murk surrounding the Blenheim, land emerged. There was no alternative but to attempt an emergency forced landing. It was successfully carried out. The Blenheim had alighted on land belonging to a cottage known as Tyddyn Rhydderch near Aberffraw Common. The only casualty was the Air Gunner, who had minor injuries to his back and knees. Close to the site of the emergency landing there was a school and in no time the downed Blenheim became the cynosure of a crowd of excited, curious schoolchildren. The three members of the crew were taken to Rhosneigr, then to RAF Penrhos, near Pwllheli and from there returned to Bicester on the following day. Their aircraft was not a write-off and after being repaired it flew again, though its life was to be short. Only twelve months later, on 8 April 1941, it crashed at RAF Church Fenton, Yorkshire. Many years after the Aberffraw incident, the Blenheim's Air Gunner returned permanently to Anglesey – he had chosen, upon his retirement, to take up residence in Rhosneigr.

Supermarine Spitfire, L1034, Beaumaris, 13 March 1941

This aircraft was from No.57 OTU, based at RAF Hawarden, Flintshire, and on that March day was being flown by a 21-year old Canadian pilot. Whilst flying over the eastern part of Anglesey the Spitfire became uncontrollable and the pilot baled out. He landed in trees close to Gallows Point, just outside the town of Beaumaris, leaving the Spitfire to its fate. The machine remained airborne for a brief period before crashing in the middle of the town.

A major disaster could so easily have arisen from this event but mercifully Beaumaris, an attractive and historical place, was to be spared such a calamity. No person was hurt or killed though there was damage to property – a grocery shop known as Gwalia Stores and an adjoining house were severely damaged and set on fire after the aircraft plunged through their roofs. The Spitfire's pilot was eventually located, and found to be hanging from his parachute, whose lines were caught in the branches of a tree. Having watched his aircraft fall on the town, his first words to his rescuers were, 'Have I killed anyone?' A colourfully embroidered account of this crash can be found in Winifred Brown's *No Distress Signals* (London, 1952, pp 66-68).

Gwalia Stores was repaired after the crash of the Spitfire and continued in business, (and still does so at the time of writing, 2000). A few yards along the street was the junior section of the Beaumaris Secondary Modern School, of which educational establishment the author was a pupil in the mid 1950s. Every lunchtime, he and hordes of other schoolchildren would descend upon Gwalia Stores, which was the school's tuck-shop. Lunchtimes must have been the shopkeeper's busiest (and surely most lucrative) period, with his shop filled to the door, and beyond, with noisy children eager to spend their money on sweets, crisps and soft drinks. When faced with this daily tidal upsurge of custom – and profit – the shopkeeper was hard put to take the many tuppences, threepences and sixpences that were pushed into his hand, and at the same time keep an eagle-eye open for pilferers! But, one wonders, how many of those schoolchildren knew of the drama at Gwalia Stores in 1941? Certainly, the author remained in ignorance of the event until well into adulthood.

Bristol Beaufighter T3024, 15 November 1941

Beaufighter T3024 was an aircraft flown by No.456 (RAAF)

Squadron, based at RAF Valley. This particular squadron had been formed at Valley in June 1941 and was the station's resident night fighter unit. On 15 November 1941 T3024 was being piloted by a Sergeant pilot when he misjudged his landing approach and struck sand dunes, (Valley had been built in an area of coastal sand dunes). Landing on one wheel and a wingtip the Beaufighter slid along the gound, bending the machine's propellers and breaking off the undercarriage. This was a typical example of many a landing accident seen at Anglesey's three airfields during the course of the war. Indeed, the next such accident occurred only a few days later . . .

Bristol Beaufighter R2372, 20 November 1941

On this day R2372 was being landed when the aircraft swung to port and the pilot found himself heading straight towards the wreckage of T3024. He increased the port engine's RPM to correct the swing and as the aircraft straightened, the stresses imposed upon the port undercarriage were too much and it collapsed, allowing the Beaufighter to skid along the runway, severing a wingtip and a propeller in the process.

Bristol Beaufighter R2474, 5 January 1942, (4.45 p.m.)

The first of three of 456 Squadron's Beaufighters which came to grief within the space of a few hours. A newly-arrived flying instructor and an US Army Signal Corps officer, serving with the squadron, were carrying out an air test with practise AI homings to Valley, when, on one of these approaches the pilot allowed his airspeed to get too low and the aircraft stalled and spun into the sea. The Beaufighter hit the water near the Old Lifeboat House, Rhosneigr. Details given in the subsequent crash report are thus:

> ASR response came from 275 Sqdn at Valley, who scrambled on their first mission since becoming operational. Two

Lysanders carried out searches over the sea off Rhosneigr though Sgt Lee had to abandon his attempt with engine trouble and subsequently made a forced landing near Aberdaron [on the Llŷn Peninsula and *thirty miles* from the crash scene. Could the report's compiler have mistaken Aberdaron for Aberffraw? The latter is a coastal village only three miles or so from Rhosneigr]. Sgt Hopkinson succeeded in locating the Beaufighter but could find no trace of the crew. In spite of this he dropped a dinghy on the spot in the hope that it might be of some use to an unseen survivor. F/Lt Hamlyn then arrived upon the scene in the Walrus, but was waved away by the crew of a HS [High Speed] Launch which had already picked up the body of [the American officer]. The Walrus then returned to base.

The crashed Beaufighter's pilot remained missing and his body had, in fact, drifted south for some fifty miles before being eventually recovered, ten days later, from the sea near Pwllheli.

Bristol Beaufighter T3028, 5 January 1942, (7.55 p.m.)

Three hours after the fatal accident to R2474, the pilot of T3028 undershot whilst landing on a very dark night and struck the Glide Path Indicator lights with his tailwheel.

Bristol Beaufighter R2476, 5 January 1942 (8.55 p.m.)

It was only an hour later when 456 Squadron suffered its *third* accident of the evening. Beaufighter R2476 was coming in to land, and as the pilot selected flaps down in preparation for the landing, the port outer flap failed (because of a broken turnbuckle in the actuating mechanism) and the aircraft lurched to starboard. Unfortunately, there was insufficient height to correct this sudden movement and the aircraft came down in a muddy field at Trewan Sands, one and a half miles from Valley. The crew escaped but the aircraft was a write-off. From a flight safety viewpoint, the evening of 5 January had been one of 456's worst. (See also Chapter 6, which tells of another accident involving a 456 Squadron Beaufighter).

Hawker Sea Hurricane P3452, 26 January 1942

On 26 January forty-year old Lt. Robert W.H. Everett, DSO, RNVR, of 801 Squadron, Fleet Air Arm, flew the squadron's hack, a worn-out Sea Hurricane, (P3452), from Belfast to Abingdon for a major inspection. The take-off was at 12.30 p.m. but the aircraft never reached its destination. At 1.15 p.m. the Coastguard officer at Penmon, Anglesey, received a message from a Coast Watcher at Red Wharf Bay that an aircraft had come down in the Bay. The aircraft was approaching from a northerly direction, losing height and with the engine making 'banging noises'. It was clear that the pilot's intention was to make an emergency landing on the beach, but at the last moment the stricken machine dived into the sea. High speed ASR (Air Sea Rescue) launches from Holyhead and Menai Bridge raced to the scene, as did the Moelfre lifeboat, which was only five miles away. However, the sea was rough and it was not until 3.20 p.m. that the sunken aircraft was finally located, lying in three fathoms of water. There was no sign of the pilot, whose harness was undone. This fact proved that he had survived the impact with the water and had managed to escape from the cockpit. A search for him continued until darkness fell, though nothing was recovered except a few personal items – a sponge bag and shaving kit – and an aircraft panel. 'No more information received' stated the Coastguard's log.

Eventually, divers went down at low water to the submerged Hurricane and used air bags to lift the aircraft. When Everett's body was washed ashore several weeks later a post-mortem examination showed that he had drowned. He was buried at Llanddona churchyard. His DSO had been awarded because he was the first pilot from a CAM-ship, the *Maplin*, to shoot down an enemy aircraft, a Focke-Wulf Condor, in August 1941. Besides this military achievement, Everett could claim another distinction; in peacetime he was a well-known jockey and in 1929 rode Gregalach, the winner of that year's Grand National Steeplechase. Everett also won the Irish Grand National Steeplechase in 1934.

Bristol Beaufighter T3026, 30 January 1942

This aircraft, flown by the same pilot who had flown Beaufighter R2476 when it crashed on 5 January, landed with its undercarriage up.

Bristol Beaufighter T3012, 20 March 1942

In this incident, the pilot (only on his third solo in a Beaufighter) was taking off when his aircraft began to swing to port. This was a well known characteristic of Beaufighters which Pilot's Notes referred to in its advice on take-off technique; ' . . . It is essential to raise the tail as early as possible. It will be found that there is a strong tendency to swing to port, but this may be corrected by coarse use of the rudder.' In the case of T3012, the pilot, when he attempted to correct the swing that was developing, unfortunately over-corrected. As a result the aircraft swung wildly in the opposite direction. Instead of breaking free from his difficulties, the pilot was now deeper in trouble than ever and was on the verge of losing control of his aircraft because of these oscillations. He then made a desparate bid to become airborne, a bid which failed when the Beaufighter's port wing struck a windsock post. This post was made of steel and ripped off the wing of the aircraft. Minus its port wing, the machine fell and slid along the ground for 300 yards before bursting into flames.

The pilot, who remained uninjured at this point, tried to escape through the hatch located on the top of the cockpit canopy but the hatch had become jammed. Denied this exit, the pilot was forced to take a much riskier line of escape by pushing through a large gash torn in the side of the fuselage during the ground slide, the risk arising out of the fact that the fuselage was on fire. The flames inflicted second-degree burns to the man's face and hands. He spent the next month in hospital having these burns treated.

As for the Beaufighter, it was, of course, a complete write-off. Its destruction was recorded thus in the Squadron's Operations Record Book; 'The aircraft provided a spectacular fireworks display, a "Brocks Benefit" [Brocks were the manufacturers of fireworks] as cannon shells [exploded] and [fuel] tanks burnt. The Fire Engine was unable to do anything because of flying shrapnel, and so covered itself with foam instead (due to airman manipulating hose and inadvertently turning it towards the engine!)'

Bristol Beaufighter R2381, 2 May 1942

Another accident when the take-off swing of a Beaufighter had not been corrected and the aircraft ran off the runway. A new, unpractised pilot was at the controls. The Station Commander was not pleased with what had happened. 'To continue training the inexperienced pilots we are receiving would be a waste of life, aircraft and national effort', he wrote.

Bristol Beaufighter X8205, 14 September 1942

This 456 Squadron aircraft was being flown over Anglesey when the starboard engine's performance became erratic and after a period of rough running it stopped completely. The pilot descended through overcast and made a wheels-up forced landing in a field belonging to Craig Fawr farm, Penmynydd. The landing was not entirely successful as the Beaufighter collided with a stone wall, which it penetrated, and then hit a second wall which brought the machine to a halt. A fire started in the port engine while the crew hurriedly vacated the aircraft. They ran for about fifty yards and crouched behind a wall as the Beaufighter quickly became engulfed in flames and burnt out. The pilot wrote, ' . . . by the time we were rescued all that was left was a pile of white manganese dust in the profile of a Beaufighter.'

Hawker Henley L3301, 26 September 1942

Hawker Henley L3301 belonged to 'J' Flight of No.1 Anti-Aircraft Cooperation Unit, RAF Bodorgan. The aircraft carried a crew of two: the pilot and a winch operator. The crash report reads: 'First sortie of the day. The machine made a low pass over the gun-park at Tŷ Croes [a Royal Artillery camp close to Bodorgan], struck one of the guns [a 3.7 AA gun] and crashed out of control into the sea. 275's Walrus [No.275 Squadron was an Air Sea Rescue unit based at RAF Valley] was scrambled at 10.10 [a.m.] to search the west coast of Anglesey. They found wreckage off the shore at Bodorgan. F/S [Flight Sergeant] Smith landed to search for survivors but none were found. A glove and an oxygen mask were picked up, and also part of the wreckage, which included the Henley's number. The Walrus then turned back to base.' There was no sign of the missing crew but three months later, on 14 December, the body of the Henley's winch operator was washed up on the beach at Cable Bay, two miles north of the crash location.

This accident resulted from a 'beat-up', euphemistically referred to in the official report as a 'low pass', that went wrong. Artillery cooperation – providing target practice for gunners, usually by means of towed drogues – was more often than not a tedious form of flying and a beat-up of gun emplacements was a favourite way of injecting a little excitement into the proceedings. Fine judgement of speed and height was called for, and it was easy to make a mistake. Such beat-ups could prove fatal, as in this case.

de Havilland Mosquito DZ658, 25 January 1943

This aircraft undershot badly when approaching Valley at night and skidded across the railway line which runs along the eastern boundary of the airfield, leaving a wheel on the track. The crew were unhurt. A few minutes later a train hit the wheel but no further damage or injuries resulted.

de Havilland Tiger Moth T7612, 9 November 1943 (3.15 p.m.)

Two Sergeant pilots from RAF Bodorgan were killed when their Tiger Moth crashed near the village of Llangaffo, three miles from the airfield. The two pilots had indulged in that dangerous but stimulating sport – unauthorised low flying.

Avro Anson MG627, 15 January 1944

This Anson was from RAF Llandwrog, near Caernarfon. Piloted by a Flying Officer R.T. Thornton, it force landed at Tynygongl and was badly damaged though the crew members were unhurt. Many forced landings occurred in Anglesey during the war.

Miles Martinet HP183, 8 February 1944 (11.55 a.m.)

The aircraft was from 1606 Flight, RAF Bodorgan and was flown by a 22-year old Sergeant pilot. He was engaged on artillery cooperation with guns located at Gorsgoch, Holyhead, when, during a 'beat-up' of these guns his aircraft crashed into them and he was killed. This was a similar accident to that of Hawker Henley L3301, previously referred to. The official record of the Gorsgoch crash gave the cause as 'unauthorised low flying'.

Miles Martinet MS784 & de Havilland Mosquito HK752, 11 February 1944 (3.40 p.m.)

The Mosquito, from 125 Squadron, collided with a drogue being towed by the Martinet, which was based at RAF Bodorgan. The latter aircraft was performing artillery cooperation duties with the RA camp at Tŷ Croes, a few miles from Bodorgan, when the collision occurred. Although the Mosquito lost seven feet from its starboard wing in the accident it still landed safely at Valley – a tribute to the skills of the pilot and the flying qualities of the Mosquito.

Douglas C-47 Dakota, 2 September 1944

This US Air Force aircraft was making an emergency landing at Valley with its starboard engine on fire. During the final approach the engine became detached from its mountings and fell with a mighty thud only fifty yards from the clubhouse of the Rhosneigr Golf Club. The aircraft, meanwhile, continued with its approach to Valley, where it crash landed and was burnt out. None of the crew was injured.

Avro Anson N9911, 16 May 1945 (1.30 a.m.)

The Anson was from RAF Llandwrog and crashed while attempting a night landing at RAF Mona. Of the four-man crew, three were killed and one seriously injured.

With the end of the Second World War, the level of flying activity in Anglesey dropped dramatically and with it so did the accidents. Never again would the island's airspace be utilised so intensely for flying and never again, thankfully, would there be so many crashes and broken bodies lying within the mangled, twisted wreckage of aircraft.

- 11 -

Vampire Ditchings and Crashes

Royal Air Force Valley's period of post-war doldrums came to
an end early in 1951 when the airfield was given a significant
new role; it was to become a base for the advanced training of
jet pilots. For this purpose No.202 Advanced Flying School
(AFS) was to be formed at the airbase. The School was intended
to provide an intermediate step for trainee aircrew between
Flying Training Schools and Operational Training Units, thereby
ensuring a smoother transition from the relative simplicity of
training aircraft to the demanding complexity of operational
types. To train its students 202 AFS was equipped with twin-
seat Meteor T.7s and single-seat Vampire FB5s. The former were
used to provide initial instruction in jet handling whilst the
latter were used for solo flying.

On 12 April the seven pilots who made up No.1 Course
assembled at Valley. All were airborne in Meteors for the first
time on the 18th and all had soloed on Vampires by the 26th.
These men were to become the first of a long line of Valley-
trained aviators – a line which was to stretch to the end of the
century and beyond, and a line which included not only RAF
and Fleet Air Arm pilots but those from foreign and
Commonwealth Air Forces also.

In the autumn of 1952 the unit's tandem-seat Meteors were
progressively replaced by Vampire T.11s, which had side-by-
side seating. The change-over was a slow process, as the unit's
Operations Record Book comments; 'numerous teething
troubles are being experienced' – for instance, failures of the fuel
system, slightly unpredictable spin characteristics and a
proneness for canopies to shatter. Interestingly, although the
seating arrangement of the T.11 made for companionship and
ease of instructing, once the Vampire's period of service ended

at Valley, the RAF reverted to tandem seating in its replacement advanced jet trainer, the Gnat. It was felt that tandem seating gave students a better feel for the operational aircraft they would eventually fly.

With the arrival of jets in Anglesey's airspace accidents began to occur, and continued to do so throughout the twelve-year period of the Vampire's dominance at Valley. There were at least sixty recorded incidents in Anglesey (with most centred on Valley itself, as one would expect) and there were further incidents further afield, in the mountains of Snowdonia, for example, but to list every single incident would be exaustingly repetive and tiresome in the extreme. Therefore, only some accidents are described, relatively briefly, in the hope that the imperfect picture which results will, nevertheless, be viewed as one that tells most of the story of Vampire accidents in Anglesey. A few of these accidents have involved ditchings and as the Vampire was considered an aircraft extremely difficult, if not impossible to ditch, some fascinating stories have resulted.

Vampire ditchings

Until 31 July 1951 no pilot had successfully ditched a Vampire. Even attempting to do so was officially disapproved and so, in line with this view, the advice given in Pilot's Notes was to bale out.

> The ditching characteristics are *believed* [author's italics] to be poor due to the probability of the tail booms hitting the water, causing a nose-down pitch and subsequent dive-in, or the tail booms may break off. It is recommended therefore that the aircraft should be abandoned rather than ditched.

By using the word 'believe' the anonymous writer of Pilot's Notes shows that a degree of uncertainty existed as to the behaviour of a Vampire when it alighted on water. This uncertainty was reflected in the teaching given to fledgling pilots at 202 AFS. One of the School's students during the summer of 1951 was Geoffrey Siers, who recollects a somewhat inadequate briefing given to him and his fellow-students.

Now, a Vampire we were informed had never been ditched successfully, simply because the position of the air intakes was such that when the aircraft hit the sea, water would enter the intakes and pull the aeroplane down. We were told that if we got into a situation where we would have to consider ditching – don't do it, bale out instead. Then, when we asked how we got out, [the Flying Instructors] said, "We don't really know but we think the best thing to do is invert the aeroplane, trim it forward, jettison the canopy, undo the seat harness and then let go of the stick and just fall out." In other words, what they were admitting was that they were not too sure themselves but as far as we, their students, were concerned, it was a question of "figure it out for yourself and you'll probably be okay." Well, we did have a guy who figured it out for himself.

He was Pilot Officer Peter Dimmock, an ex-Cranwell cadet who, in July 1951, was undergoing training at Valley. On Tuesday the 31st he was flying Vampire WA160 in circumstances described thus by one of his colleagues.

We had a low-level cross-country run which went twice around [Anglesey]and we were then allowed down to fifty feet. The day Pete went, it was 8/8 overcast with featureless cloud, nil wind but plenty of haze. On his first passage of Red Wharf Bay [Dulas Bay, five miles to the north, is the location given in the official record] he inadvertently splashed the surface, the horizon being most indistinct. Water entered the intakes and put out the fire [the engine had flamed-out]. There was no relight system then and [Dimmock] didn't fancy baling out as this usually involved a double leg break.

He made about 1,600 feet [that is, he converted speed to height] after hitting the water but was too far from land to achieve a "feet dry" landing. There was a stationary fishing smack out in the Bay, so he headed for that, lowered twenty degrees of flap and gently touched down. Tests indicated that the tail booms would break off and the pod sink rapidly. However, the sea was calm that day, the booms remained intact and the aircraft planed almost to a halt and then sunk.

Sunk like a stone, in fact, and although the water in which the jet trainer was now immersed could not be described as forbiddingly deep, there being only thirty feet between the surface and seabed, Dimmock, nevertheless needed to have his wits about him if he was going to overcome the next problem that presented itself. How was he to escape from the sunken aircraft?

Fortunately, he obeyed the golden rule applicable in any emergency or life threatening situation if one wishes to maximise one's chances of survival; remain cool, calm and collected, and think quickly. This the resourceful pilot did. Finding himself sitting on the seabed in the pressurised cockpit of the Vampire (all of Valley's machines were flown completely pressurised from take-off to landing) and still strapped in, he methodically undid all his attachments – although he did forget to disconnect his oxygen supply, initially – unbuckled his harness straps, his parachute straps, removed his helmet, operated the de-pressurisation system, unlocked the canopy and then began to wind it back by means of the small wheel located on the starboard side of the cockpit.

But he only gave a part turn to the wheel, sufficient to open the canopy no more than a quarter of an inch or so. This was what the pilot intended because it created enough of a gap to allow the water to enter at a controlled rate and also to trap a bubble of air underneath the canopy, thereby allowing Dimmock to breathe while he waited for the rising water to flood the cockpit. When the water reached his shoulders he

116

operated the canopy jettison mechanism, inflated his Mae West*, wherupon the pilot shot to the surface in the air bubble released by the removal of the canopy.

It was a superbly executed escape during which Dimmock remained calm and clear thinking throughout. As one of his friends remarked, 'The only thing that went wrong for him was the ruin of his issue Longines watch – they were not waterproofed in those days!' Even his rescue was quick and efficient. After making his decision to ditch, Dimmock, for obvious reasons, aimed for the fishing boat, and as he wished, the Vampire came to a halt close to the boat, whose crew had, of course, witnessed the incident. When Dimmock bobbed to the surface he was spotted immediately by the boat's crew and was in the water for less than five minutes before being hauled aboard the vessel, wet but unharmed. Geoffrey Siers recollects Dimmock's arrival back at Valley.

> We were sitting outside our flight hut when this RAF truck pulled up and this guy climbed out, soaking wet, absolutely soaking wet. We found out from him what he did was actually hit the water . . . Then, because everybody was so interested in how he managed to ditch a Vampire and live to tell the tale, he spent the following six months writing reports about it!

Sadly, the next ditching ended in a very different manner. On the morning of Saturday, 24 October 1953 one of Valley's student pilots was airborne in Vampire VV226 carrying out

---

*A type of pneumatic lifejacket aptly named by RAF pilots of the Second World War after the voluptuously full-breasted Mae West, the legendary Hollywood film actress and sex symbol. Mae West was not only sexy but witty also. Upon being told that an item of flying clothing was being reverently named after her and her ample proportions, she remarked, 'It made me feel like I started a second front of my own.' Indeed, the term 'Mae West' entered *Webster's International Dictionary,* to which distinction Miss West is said to have reacted with the statement, 'I've been in *Who's Who* and I know what's what, but it'll be the first time I ever made the dictionary.'

aerobatic exercises over the sea north of Anglesey. Shortly before 10.50 a.m. the pilot passed a Mayday signal to base stating that his aircraft's engine had flamed out. The Vampire was at an altitude of 8,000 feet and 15 miles from land at the time. Following the loss of power, the student made several unsuccessful attempts to relight the engine.

At Valley the duty QFI (there has to be a flying instructor in the control tower at all times when students are airborne) gave the pilot a course to steer for land but back came the pilot's reply that he would not be able to make it. In fact, his attempt to relight the engine was an error because it wasted so much valuable time when he could have been homing towards Anglesey and he might well have reached the island if only he had set course immediately after his engine failed. Then, to compound the student's difficulties, the duty QFI, whose judgement in such circumstances was crucial, made a mistake that was to seal the student's fate. He was instructed by the QFI to prepare for a ditching rather than the officially preferred option (as already described) of baling out. Additionally, the pilot was requested to change his radio's frequency to that of the International Distress Frequency. This request was not quite understood by him and he queried it by asking, 'Do you mean Channel C?' For some unknown reason Valley did not answer this call and no further transmissions were received from the Vampire, which continued to glide seawards.

Nothing more was seen or heard of the aircraft but soon after 10.50 a.m. a disturbance was observed in the sea near the Skerries, just off the northern coastline of Anglesey. The disturbance was at the Vampire's likely point of impact in the opinion of the subsequent Board of Inquiry, and indicated a failed ditching. To quote from the Inquiry's findings; 'The pilot was wrongly advised by the Duty QFI when he was told to take emergency action, as students are taught to abandon the aircraft rather than ditch it. The responsibility for the lack of reply to the pilot's question regarding Channel C rests with the Duty QFI.'

Comments of this kind would have done little to enhance his career prospects.

After the loss of Vampire VV226 there were only two other successful ditchings of a Vampire; in December 1953, by a Norwegian Air Force pilot, who managed to put his aircraft down in Trondheim fiord, and in June 1956 by a 23-year old Royal Navy student who, as it so happened was, like Peter Dimmock, also undergoing training at Valley. On the morning of Saturday, 23 June, he took off in Vampire FB5 WA285 – his first solo in a Vampire – but soon after becoming airborne and when overflying Holyhead, his aircraft's Goblin engine failed. The jet, with the distinctively shrill whine of its engine now silenced (forever), began to lose airspeed and altitude. Heading downwards, the pilot was, unfortunately, too far from base to return and so he had to decide upon one of two alternatives; either to abandon the aircraft or attempt to ditch. He chose the latter. This decision was made because of his previous experience. He had been aboard an aircraft carrier during the Korean War and had observed a number of badly damaged aircraft make successful ditchings – observations which he felt he could now put to good use. Tilting the balance well and truly in favour of a ditching was the pilot's distaste for baling out, an action which he thought impossibly difficult in a Vampire.

He approached the sea at a location two miles north of South Stack lighthouse, jettisoned his Vampire's canopy and delayed the touch-down for as long as he could. When it became impossible to hold off the aircraft any longer, he allowed it to make contact with the water, after which the machine bounced a couple of times and sank immediately, with its occupant still in the cockpit. Submerged, the pilot undid his straps but found that his dinghy had snagged, preventing him from escaping. He freed himself from the dinghy and swam upwards, inflating his lifejacket on reaching the surface. Luckily, he had previously done some underwater swimming, which fact served him well in his present situation. He suffered only a couple of minor cuts and after thirty minutes in the water he was rescued by one of Valley's SAR Whirlwind helicopters. Thus the third, and final, successful ditching of a Vampire came to a satisfactory conclusion.

Other Vampire accidents

The majority of Vampire accidents on Anglesey soil have involved the single-seater FB5s. These small aircraft attracted some interesting comments from those who flew them. One pilot likened them to 'Dinky Toys, cuddly, compact little beasts, but you felt you were a little too close to the runway for comfort and no ejection seats either!' Another pilot said, 'When you took off and landed, you rattled down the runway on those tiny little wheels in a tiny little machine that was a sort of pram with wings.' Nevertheless, even a 'pram with wings' could bite.

Vampire FB5 VZ333, 7 June 1951

Number 202 AFS' first casualty. The aircraft hit the ground on final approach and lost its undercarriage, resulting in a belly landing on the runway. Geoffrey Siers saw this accident when he was about to become airborne and provides an eye-witness account.

One day we were using the short runway, which runs from the beach [of Cymyran] to the railway line . . . The caravan was alongside the threshold and had two fire tenders in attendance – that was the practice then. I held at the holding point whilst a student in a Vampire approached to land. He was obviously concerned about landing distance and aimed to touch down at the caravan. He undershot and hit the dunes, wrote off his gear, bent both booms upwards and also the short jet pipe, coming to a halt abeam the caravan. The fire tenders did not move, merely foaming the Vampire from their fixed positions, much to the chagrin of the pilot, who was all for hopping out!'

Vampire FB5 WA298, 2 July 1951

The unit's first fatal accident. This aircraft was being flown by a Persian officer, Captain Sirang, who, during an instrument let-down, crashed in the sea two miles off Llanddwyn. It was believed that the crash had been caused by inadvertent and extremely rapid inflation of the dinghy, which was part of the parachute pack upon which the pilot sat. Dinghy inflation in the confined space of the cockpit would have fouled the control column, pushing it forward and causing the aircraft to go into a bunt from which recovery was impossible. Once the danger of this almost instant incapacitation was realised the other pilots armed themselves (albeit unofficially) with 'dinghy-stabbers' – small knives attached to their flying suits. In the event of an accidental inflation the knife would be used to stab the dinghy, thereby deflating it and allowing control of the aircraft to be regained.

For an interesting discussion of this subject, in relation to the loss of Supermarine Attacker WA485 in February 1952 and the development of 'dinghy-stabbing' see *Aeroplane Monthly*, June 1997, pp18-20. The magazine article claims that, 'The first known occasion on which an inadvertent dinghy inflation in a jet aircraft had occurred was when a Meteor F.4 was lost while being flown from No.226 Operational Conversion Unit at Stradishall on October 25, 1951.' This was three months after the loss of WA298 at Valley. Today a multi-purpose knife forms an integral part of the sophisticated flying suit that is worn by all Service aircrew.

Vampire FB5 VV547, 21 December 1951

This aircraft was being landed by a student when the brakes

failed and the pilot selected undercarriage 'up' to avoid overshooting. It was the first of two accidents that day for 202 AFS.

Gloster Meteor T.7 WA716, 21 December 1951

The second accident involved a 'meatbox', (a nickname given to Meteors). It was being flown by a QFI and his student when, because of fuel mismanagement, the aircraft's tanks began to run dry. In an attempt to reach base, the QFI flew the Meteor on one engine but this was not successful and a forced landing had to be carried out. The location was Malltraeth Marsh, eleven miles south-east of Valley. No injuries resulted to the crew but the aircraft was badly damaged.

Vampire FB5 WE835, 19 March 1953

The aircraft overshot during an emergency landing, scattering wreckage for a distance of a quarter of a mile. The pilot was killed.

Vampire FB5 WA134, 9 July 1953

The Libyan pilot of this aircraft attempted to bale out when he got into an inverted spin but there was insufficient height for his parachute to deploy fully and he was killed. The Vampire crashed on, and set fire to, outbuildings belonging to Nantannog Farm, Llanerchymedd, injuring several pigs to the extent that they had to be destroyed.

Vampire T.11 WZ561, 7 January 1954

On Thursday, 7 January, shortly after 4.00 p.m. WZ561 took off with an NCO instructor and his student on board. Some twenty minutes later, whilst at a height of 15,000 feet over Anglesey, the aircraft got into a spin. The spin continued until the Vampire was only a few hundred feet above the ground. At this low height the hood was jettisoned prior to the occupants abandoning the aircraft. The student escaped but his parachute did not open and he was killed when he hit the ground. Later investigation showed there had been no attempt to open the parachute, suggesting that the student might well have been incapacitated during the bale out. His instructor remained with the aircraft until it crashed and he too was killed. The accident occurred near the village of Pentraeth, the closest dwelling to the crash site being a house known as Tanrallt.

The poor spin recovery characteristics of the Vampire were well known and in an attempt to improve the situation, aircraft were fitted with six-foot dorsal fairings which extended along the tail booms. Following the accident to WZ561 Pilot's Notes were amended, allowing four turns in an aircraft fitted with fairings and up to two turns in aircraft not so fitted. The recommended altitude of 6,000 feet for abandoning the aircraft remained.

One of the RAF's tasks, after an aircraft crash, is to remove the resultant wreckage – often a thoroughly unpleasant job. Wreckage removal was the responsibility of Maintenance Units, in this particular case No.1 MU, based at Stafford. Large transporters of a type known as 'Queen Marys' were used to convey wreckage from a site and it so happened that the 'Queen Mary' driver allocated to the Pentraeth crash was a North Walian, an Anglesey man, in fact, and we can let him tell his story in his own words.

In the 1950s I did my National Service as an MT driver in the RAF. I drove a 'Queen Mary' at No.1 MU. Part of my duties included attendance at aircraft crash sites where the 'Queen Mary' would be used to transport wreckage, usually back to the base camp of the crashed aircraft. I drove to all parts of the UK during the time I did this job and I took part in many crash salvage operations. It was not enjoyable work.

One day in January 1954 our unit received a call from RAF Valley, as there had been a crash in Anglesey. We set off for North Wales immediately. Normally, I would drive to the station which had requested our unit's services, in order to find out the precise location of the crash site but in this case, as I knew Anglesey well (having been born and bred in the village of Pentraeth) I thought it would be a good idea, to save time, if I found out the exact location first, so that I could drive straight there. Imagine my surprise when I was told that my destination was a house named Tanrallt, near Pentraeth – it was my own home!

At the crash site itself it was a gruesome, horrible job having to search for human remains around the crater caused by the impact but once the SMO [Station Medical Officer] and other medics were satisfied that all human remains had been removed and the crash investigators had looked at the site we could then begin the job of clearing the wreckage. Walls and hedges had to be demolished to get a crane and the 'Queen Mary' to the site. We then set about picking up every piece of wreckage, down to the tiniest scrap, for transportation back to Valley. Once this job was completed we had to make good the damage we had caused to property. The whole operation, from the time of leaving Stafford to repairing the last wall, took about ten days to complete. During this period I was able to live at home, which made a very nice and acceptable change from living in a tent, which I sometimes had to endure on this kind of trip.

Vampire FB5 WA307, 16 July 1954

This aircraft crashed at RAF Mona during unauthorised low-level aerobatics. The pilot, of Polish nationality, attempted a roll, misjudged it and collided with the ground. He was killed instantly.

Vampire FB5 VV659, 16 November 1954

On this day VV659 was being flown by a student pilot engaged on a solo aerobatic exercise to the west of Valley. The official record states that, 'During the detail the aircraft got into a spin from a stall turn and being unable to recover, the pilot abandoned the aircraft. A successful descent into the sea [at Cymyran Bay] was made and the pilot was later picked up by the DUKW amphibious vehicle from [Valley]. The aircraft crashed near Rhoscolyn, in a marsh.'

Omitted from the record is the fact that a race to rescue the pilot had developed – a race between the DUKW and a small boat. The boat had set off from Cymyran beach and was rowed by Ernest Naish, whom readers will recall was the man who helped the fatally injured Dr Chill after the crash of a Wellington bomber near Bodedern in 1943 (as described in Chapter 8). Since 1951 Naish had been the manager of the Fairey Aviation guided weapons development unit at Valley, a job which he combined with the husbandry of his Bodedern farm.

The Fairey site was located at the southern end of the airfield, adjacent to Cymyran beach, where on that November day Naish happened to spot the Vampire's pilot descending into the sea. Naish immediately launched the boat and, in his own words, 'rowed like hell!', hoping to get to the downed pilot before the DUKW. The boat's occupant was young and strong and a powerful rower but he could not compete against the DUKW, although it gave him much satisfaction to be beaten by a few yards only. On the other hand, he was most put out not to be offered a tow back the beach by the DUKW's crew!

Vampire FB5 VV554, 31 December 1955

On 21 November 1955 a group of pilots trained in Canada arrived at Valley to form No.20 Canadian Acclimatisation Course, the purpose of the course being, as the name suggests, to acclimatise the pilots to the very different conditions met within UK airspace in comparison to that of Canada. Sadly, it was the somewhat inadequate design of the Vampire FB5 cockpit canopy which was to cause the death of one of these men on the last day of the year.

The pilot in question had taken off to carry out an aerobatic sortie but soon afterwards his aircraft was seen diving into a field belonging to Trescawen Home Farm, three miles north of Llangefni. The aircraft exploded on impact and the pilot was killed. He had baled out but his parachute was torn off in the process. The shroud lines showed evidence of having been scorched, as if by jet efflux, which then caused them to snap when strained. The Board of Inquiry into the accident concluded that the cockpit canopy either burst or moved backwards when the aircraft was at high speed, causing damage to the tailplane and resulting in loss of control. 'Mod 3506 is well advanced to fit an improved canopy on the Vampire 5' stated the accident record card, though the modification would come too late for one unfortunate pilot.

Vampire FB5 WG835, 29 January 1957

This aircraft, piloted by a 24-year old Naval student, lost power when taking off from Valley's runway 02. The pilot responded to the emergency by raising the undercarriage in an attempt to stop the Vampire, but it overshot across the public road close to the runway. Whenever aircraft are in the process of taking off or landing here, road traffic is halted, for obvious safety reasons, by means of lights operated from the control tower. During this particular take-off the lights, as usual, were on red, bringing a number of cars to a stop, and it was towards the first vehicle in this line that the Vampire swung as it careered off the runway. A collision was only narrowly avoided. Beyond the road is an area of marshland and small lakes where reeds grow in abundance and into which vegetation the out-of-control Vampire hurtled. It came to a halt right side up, facing the way it had come and in a partly submerged condition.

The tall, thick-growing reeds had, most probably, saved the pilot's life by absorbing much of the force of the crash. He climbed out of the cockpit unhurt and managed to reach the safety of solid ground without even getting wet, thanks to RAF rescuers who extended a ladder from the lake's edge to the Vampire!

Vampire FB9 WP993, 12 December 1957

When it crashed, this aircraft was being flown by a 23-year old Naval student, who was due to graduate only seven days later. He lost control of the Vampire in a formation loop, radioed a distress call to base but was killed when the jet crashed onto farm buildings near Marianglas. A barn containing fifty tons of hay was set on fire and destroyed.

Vampire T.11 XD620, 8 August 1962

This aircraft crashed into a cottage at Rhostrehwfa near Llangefni. The pilot was killed. Inside the cottage were two elderly sisters, one of whom was confined to a wheelchair. The women were about to have lunch when their meal was disturbed by the Vampire, which demolished part of their centuries-old cottage. A fire broke out but it was soon extinguished by neighbours of the sisters. Both women were shocked but otherwise unhurt. They had been very lucky not to have suffered injury or worse.

Vampire T.11 WZ612, 24 April 1963

The aircraft's undercarriage collapsed on landing at RAF Valley. It was the last Vampire accident in Anglesey.

By the summer of 1963 the Vampire era was at an end at Valley. Thereafter, the sight and sound of Vampires in Anglesey's skies would become a thing of the past. No longer would those distinctive twin tail booms be seen or the shrill, banshee-like wail of the aircraft's Goblin jet engine be heard. A replacement aircraft, the Gnat, was already present at Valley, and had been, in small numbers, since November 1962. The Gnat suffered its share of accidents too, as will be revealed in Chapter 16.

- 12 -

The Flying Dutchmen

If the principal keeper of Start Point lighthouse, just above the drowned village of Hallsands, Devon, happened to be looking out to sea at 4.30 p.m. on the afternoon of Tuesday, 19 May 1953, as well he might, then he would have seen a very large ship located three miles from land. The vessel had a long and completely flat deck, with its superstructure located amidships – the distinctive shape and form of an aircraft carrier, in other words. This ship was, in fact, HMS *Illustrious*, one of the Royal Navy's carriers. The lighthouse keeper would also, at that particular moment, have seen three aircraft take off from the vessel and head northwards towards the coast. It would not be unreasonable for us to assume that the man, by virtue of his job, took an interest in maritime affairs but a similar interest in aviation on his part cannot be safely assumed. If, nonetheless, we imagine that he, or indeed any of the other keepers at Start Point lighthouse were knowledgeable about aviation, they would have identified the aircraft as Hawker Sea Furies. If we imagine further that one of these men had trained a pair of binoculars on the approaching Sea Furies, the observer would not have seen Fleet Air Arm markings on the aircraft. These were not British machines – they were Dutch, and displayed the markings of the Royal Netherlands Naval Air Service. They belonged to No.3 Squadron of that Service and were in the UK to carry out joint exercises with the Navy. Whilst in Britain the Dutch aircraft and their pilots were based at RNAS Anthorn, a naval air station near Carlisle and it was to this base the Sea Furies were returning that afternoon. However, what was impossible for our assumed watcher to know – and anyone else connected with the flight for that matter – was that two of the three Dutch pilots were flying to their doom.

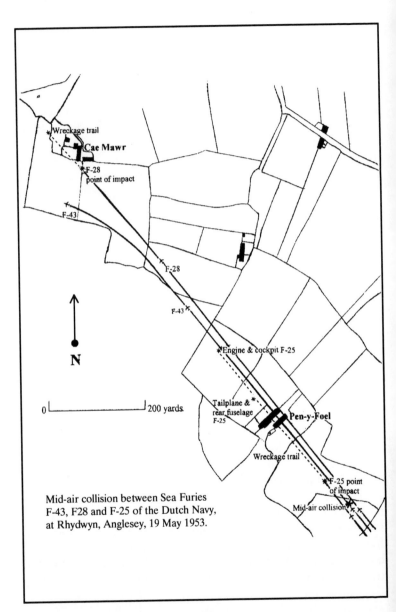

Wreckage trail

Cae Mawr

*F-28
point of impact

F-43

F-28

F-43

N

0 ————————— 200 yards

*Engine & cockpit F-25

Tailplane &
rear fuselage
F-25

Pen-y-Foel

Wreckage trail

*F-25 point
of impact

Mid-air collision

Mid-air collision between Sea Furies
F-43, F28 and F-25 of the Dutch Navy,
at Rhydwyn, Anglesey, 19 May 1953.

On board the *Illustrious* during the course of that day a number of pilots, including the three Dutchmen, had been practising deck landings – that most difficult of naval flying skills. Exponents say that to be able to do it well is what sorts the men from the boys. Be that as it may, by 4.00 p.m. that afternoon's exercises were over for the Dutch pilots and so their leader had a decision to make: whether to stay aboard the ship for the night or fly back to Anthorn. He chose the latter option despite weather conditions that were not good. It was a fateful decision which, in the event, would bring disaster to his Flight.

But before we come to that disaster, it is necessary to provide some more details of the aircraft involved and the men who flew them. The Sea Furies in question were Mark FB11s (single seat carrier-borne fighter-bombers), serial numbers F-25, F-28 and F-43. The trio's leader, a 32-year old Lieutenant piloted F-43, with a 26-year old Lieutenant in F-28 and a Sub-Lieutenant of the same age piloting F-25. As regards their flying experience, it was not extensive. The leader had a total of 1,394 hours, with 397 of those on type, whilst his subordinates were relatively unseasoned flyers – each with only a few hundred hours to his credit. The pilot of F-25 had 450 hours, with 42.30 on type and his colleague in F-28 could claim 410 hours, with 42 on type. Thus, the younger men's experience of the Sea Fury was limited.

Having decided to return to Anthorn, the senior Dutch officer had first to obtain flight authorisation and so he paid a visit to the ship's Operations Officer (of Lt. Commander rank), whose responsibility it was to perform this function. In authorising the flight, he briefed the pilot to fly at 6,000 feet 'from Start Point to Liverpool direct and from there coastwise to Anthorn . . . ' Next, the Dutch pilot went to see the Meteorological Officer, (also of Lt. Commander rank), who spoke of a cold front, 'about eighty miles wide, lying roughly from Cardiff to the North.' The cloud top 'was at 15,000 feet and base at 700 feet to 1,000 feet', said the weather man, advising the enquirer to fly underneath the cloud and follow the coast northwards. This advice, it will be noted, was in contrast to that given by the Operations Officer. The pilot, satisfied that he could still complete the flight in the poor conditions prevailing, left and headed towards his aircraft but before doing so he asked for an 'actual' weather report (as opposed to a forecast) for Anthorn. This report showed there was a substantial amount of low cloud in the region: total cloud cover at 2,500 feet, 3/8 cover at 850 feet and visibility at 4.8 miles. It did not cause the pilot to change his mind because, he said, Anthorn was 'an easy place to find' and furthermore he had 'flown a lot in this area'.

At this point, it must be made clear that the details of the flight planning briefing and authorisation thus given are only the bare bones of events that were later to become the subject of intense scrutiny by the Admiralty. A number of confusions, inadequacies and lax procedures were brought to light by subsequent inquiries – for example, the conflicting advice given by the Operations Officer and the Meteorological Officer on the route to be followed by the pilot – but to enter into detail here would serve little purpose except to bog down the narrative in a lengthy and complicated discussion of Naval flight planning procedures. Suffice it to say that the quality of the flight planning and meteorological briefings given to the pilot were later found wanting and had these briefings been properly conducted there is little doubt that the flight would not have been approved.

At 4.30 p.m. the Sea Furies took off from HMS *Illustrious* in good weather (25 miles visibility, 1/8 cumulus cloud at 2,000 feet) and headed northwards in a V formation with F-25 on the leader's port side and F-28 on his starboard. The 284-mile journey to Anthorn was planned to take two hours, the ETA being, therefore, 6.30 p.m. An 'Airmove' departure signal was sent from *Illustrious* to the aircraft's destination but for some reason or another this signal was delayed and Anthorn did not learn of the flight until half an hour after the accident had taken place. Upon becoming airborne, the three aircraft climbed to

3,000 feet until they came to the Bristol Channel, where the leader could see what he described as 'a solid mass of cloud' in front of him. It could have been a good time to turn back but he chose to continue. The cloud mass necessitated a descent to below its base, at 800 feet. After reaching South Wales, the coastline was followed to Swansea whereupon the Flight climbed to 2,000 feet and crossed the south-west corner of Wales (Pembrokeshire) in cloud – in other words, flying in Instrument Meteorological Conditions (IMC). This meant that whilst the leader was concentrating on the instruments in his cockpit in order to fly his aircraft, his two wingmen were concentrating equally hard on the difficult task of keeping formation in cloud. It was vital for them not to lose visual contact with their leader because if they did so, there was little chance of re-formating in cloud. They would then, effectively, be on their own.

Over Cardigan Bay, the Dutch trio descended to below the cloudbase, which was at 350 feet. From that point onwards the Welsh coast was followed, with the cloud gradually lowering as the aircraft progressed northwards. By the time Anglesey was reached – an hour and twenty minutes into the flight – the cloudbase was down to 250 feet. Upon sighting the island, the leader checked his map for any hills and the highest he could see was 500 feet.* He then climbed, he said, 'in cloud to about 900 or 1,000 feet, intending to cross Anglesey and letting down in the Irish Sea.' However, the leader's statement about his altitude is contradicted by a witness, and a very reliable one at that – a senior RAF officer.

Between 5.50 p.m. and 5.55 p.m. that evening Wing Commander Harold Cox, the Wing Commander (Administration) at RAF Valley, was driving his car along the A5 road, two miles from the airfield, when he saw the Sea Furies flying in V formation and heading 'approximately north'. The

*The three highest points in Anglesey are Holyhead Mountain, 722 feet/220 metres, Mynydd Bodafon, 584 feet/178 metres and Mynydd y Garn, 558 feet/170 metres. The crash occurred less than a mile from the latter.

Wing Commander estimated their height to be 'between 100 and 200 feet'. There was little doubt that they were not at '900 or 1,000 feet' as claimed by the leader, otherwise they would have been hidden by low cloud from the eyes of Wing Commander Cox. He said that visibility was one mile and there was also a slight drizzle but he did not particularly notice the cloud base, he admitted, though he was sure that it was low.

In fact, the weather for that Tuesday, as forecast by Valley's Met Office was, 'Cloudy or overcast with continuous rain or drizzle becoming intermittent at 1300 GMT [Greenwich Mean Time] for the rest of the day.' It was an accurate forecast, as revealed by Valley's 'actual', compiled at 5.00 p.m., which showed there was an overcast with slight mist, visibility at three miles, and the cloud cover was described as '8/8 Stratus at 300 feet'. This meant that the entire sky was obscured by uniform layers of low cloud. The wind was westerly and blew at a strength of twenty knots.

Wing Commander Cox continued with his car journey, little realising that two of the aircraft he had seen would crash within a few minutes, killing their pilots, whilst the third aircraft would land at the airfield whose administration Cox was in charge of, and that he, Cox, would become a witness at a Board of Inquiry.

The story now requires the introduction of a second – and female – Anglesey inhabitant, who also became a player in the drama that was about to unfold, though in a more direct way than Wing Commander Cox. Indeed, she very nearly lost her life because of the crash. She is Miss Christiana Jones, of Cae Mawr farm, near Rhydwyn. What happened to her that day is an excellent example of the 'riskiness' that is inherent in life and to which all of us are inescapably exposed by virtue of our existence. Sometimes, whether we live or die is dependent upon nothing more than random chance or the most seemingly inconsequential of decisions each of us makes daily. As the writer and poet Dylan Thomas said in these lines from *Under Milk Wood*:

For whether we make it
through the night or no
I'm sure is always touch and go.

Substitute 'day' for 'night' and we have an illustration of this truth in Christiana Jones' tale. Then in her late thirties, Christiana lived and worked on her father's farm, two miles from the tiny village of Rhydwyn, in the north-west corner of Anglesey. The farm is close to the coast, which here is amongst the rockiest to be found in the whole island and it was in this area, coincidentally, that Robert Loraine experienced his series of misadventures in 1910, (see Chapter 1). And if Rhydwyn proved to be Loraine's Golgotha so it proved also for two unfortunate Dutch pilots.

At 5.45 p.m. on the day of the accident Miss Jones was cleaning some milking equipment in the small dairy at Cae Mawr. Outside, the weather was dull, damp and disagreeable – curtains of vision-obscuring mist hung all the way down to the ground and a persistent drizzle of rain condensed out of the mist, imposing its wetness upon the landscape. But the drizzling amorphousness of that afternoon mattered little to the farmer's daughter – she was too intent upon her immediate task. She worked briskly at her chore, her plan being, once she had finished, to drive five miles to the village of Llanfechell, in order to have a wet battery recharged by the local garage. Wet batteries were often to be found in those households in rural areas lacking mains electricity and were used mostly to power radio sets, (the 1950s being a time, it must be remembered, when mains electricity was by no means universally available). The garage at Llanfechell, owned by a man named Currie Hughes, asked a price of 9d (4p) for battery charging, which was usually done overnight. In the event, Miss Jones would not make the trip to Llanfechell that Tuesday evening, though she would get the battery charged in circumstances she could never have imagined, as will be explained later.

Located a short distance – little more than a third of a mile –

from Cae Mawr was another farm, Pen-y-Foel, and it so happened that the farmer of this land was Miss Jones' brother, Wynne. During the afternoon of that wet, fog-bound day Wynne Jones decided, because of the bad weather, to do some indoor work and gave himself the task of thoroughly cleaning the cowshed. This he had done and by 5.00 p.m. he was in the process of milking (by hand) his nine cows, one of whom was on the point of calving. So close was the animal to giving birth that Mr Jones was afraid it might happen in the cowshed and the messiness caused by the discharge of the placenta etc. would ruin that afternoon's good work. Thus, after milking this particular cow he immediately moved her out of the shed and into an adjoining field. It was a decision which was to cost the animal its life and that of its unborn calf. Dylan Thomas' words apply to livestock as well as to humans.

Meanwhile, at Cae Mawr Christiana Jones was continuing to clean the milking equipment when she heard, in the distance, the sound of aero-engines. The sound swelled in volume, indicating the approach of aircraft but it was interrupted by a deep rumble which rapidly turned into a grinding, scrunching noise of growing intensity and before Miss Jones had time to think about the cause of this disturbance, the building she was in was rocked by an explosion nearby. Her heart pounding wildly, Miss Jones ran out of the dairy, to be greeted by a sight she will never forget: wreckage strewn everywhere, flames leaping high into the air, damaged outbuildings, trees in the orchard broken and flattened, and her elderly father (who was nearly eighty) standing in the farmyard watching, in disbelief, this nightmarish scene – a scene made all the more nightmarish because of the heavy, unreal atmosphere created by the mist. Luckily, Mr Jones was not hurt.

It was obvious to both him and his daughter that an aircraft had crashed on their farm and though they had no knowledge whatsoever, at that stage, of what type of aircraft it was or where it had come from, the machine was, of course, one of the three

Sea Furies seen only a few minutes previously by Wing Commander Cox. The crashed aircraft was, in fact, F-28. It had come down in a field close to the farm's outbuildings, ploughed along the ground until it came to a small hedge, which it went through and then, a moment later, came up against a more substantial obstacle in the form of a stone wall which separated Cae Mawr's outbuildings from the surrounding land. With tremendous force the Sea Fury smashed through this wall only a few yards from where the dairy stood. This was the impact which had shaken the building and given its occupant the fright of her life. Then the aircraft, its huge momentum still not halted, tore through a small orchard and garden, disintegrating as it did so in an explosive shower of flaming wreckage. The pilot stood no chance of surviving this maelstrom of violent destruction.

When Christiana Jones saw the point at which the aircraft had gone through the wall, she realised how close to being killed or injured she had come in those few terrifying moments of the crash. If the out-of-control machine's path along the ground had been only a few more yards further to the right, then the dairy, and not the stone wall, would have taken the full brunt of the collision. Most likely, an impact of this magnitude would bring about the building's demolition or at the very least cause severe damage, and with Miss Jones within the building she would have either lost her life or been badly injured. She came to regard her escape from such a fate as nothing short of miraculous. Just as lucky was her dog, a black Labrador, who, being chained to a post near the dairy could not escape the terror that rained down upon him. There was not a scratch upon the cowering animal, however, though he was very frightened by the thunderous noise and flames of the crash.

If we now return to Pen-y-Foel, we find that this farm had also become the scene of an accident, where another of the Sea Furies, F-25, came to grief. Wynne Jones' routine, like that of his sister, was suddenly interrupted by the roar of aircraft engines close by, followed by the screeching, tearing sounds of an impact centred more or less upon the farm itself and then the thud and thump of wreckage falling on and around the farmhouse and buildings. Jones, in similar fashion to his sister, emerged in extreme haste from an outbuilding and was able to discern, in misty conditions that reduced visibility to 'a distance of two hundred yards', aircraft wreckage on his land, in his garden, in his farmyard and a broken-off wing resting against his house. Inside the house was the farmer's eleven-year old son, Arthur, who had not been to school that day because of illness. Flying debris from the crash broke a window and penetrated, shrapnel-like, into the room where the boy was, but he was not injured. Other pieces of wreckage fell on the roof of the farmhouse causing considerable damage. In a field immediately beyond the farmhouse lay the largest, most substantial piece of the crashed Sea Fury: its complete rear fuselage, including the tailplane. This part of the aircraft had fractured in the area behind the pilot's cockpit and had come to rest in a vertical position, balanced somewhat precariously on the tailplane, in which position it remained until the site was cleared of all wreckage, some time after the accident. In another field, lying 150 yards further along the wreckage trail was the cockpit section with the pilot's body inside.

In yet another field lay the bodies of two bovine victims: the cow which had been milked only a short while previously, and in its mangled, blood-soaked carcass could be seen the unborn calf, claimed by Death even before the luckless animal had taken its first breath of Life. Because there was no post-crash fire to consume the destroyed aircraft's petrol, which had spilt from ruptured tanks onto the ground, a strong odour of fuel pervaded Pen-y-Foel and this powerful aroma became, for Arthur Jones, the farmer's young son, one of the most abiding memories of that traumatic afternoon. Over fifty years later, any talk of the accident will bring back the reek of aviation fuel to his nostrils.

What, meanwhile, had become of the third Sea Fury, the one

flown by the Flight's leader? It will be remembered that he had led his two wingmen across Anglesey, during which the aircraft were seen by Wing Commander Cox flying at a height of 'between 100 and 200 feet' and heading in a northerly direction. Shortly after this sighting the trio of Sea Furies flew into cloud. The leader's account of what happened next is told in his own words:

> While I was flying blind I suddenly felt a hit on my port wing, my plane then shot up and I needed both hands to recover. My Air Speed Indicator appeared to have jammed at 250 knots. I pushed the nose forward as I was afraid of stalling. I can remember just clearing a house before I was visual with the Irish Sea. I immediately called over the radio my number two and three but got no reply. As the plane was very difficult to keep level and a shower was coming, I decided to put my plane down as soon as possible, so I flew to Valley. I had no time to contact them on the radio and landed safely.

At Cae Mawr and Pen-y-Foel no-one was aware of the third aircraft and even if they had heard or seen it, their concern was, naturally enough, with what had happened on the ground. Once the occupants of the farms recovered from their initial shock, the immediate need, obviously, was to inform the authorities of the twin accidents and to summon help from the emergency services. There was no telephone at either farm, so Wynne Jones and his sister drove to nearby Rhydwyn, where the public telephone box was discovered to be out of order. Mr Jones then decided to drive his van to the nearest police station, at Llanfaethlu, where he contacted the village constable and took him back to the two farms. On the return journey the policeman, wishing to get to the scene of the accident without delay, said to the farmer, *'Dôs hynny fedri di!'* ('Go as fast as you can!'). Wynne Jones did his best to comply with this order, coping well with the misty weather and the natural restrictions imposed upon his speed by the narrow, twisting lanes which are a feature of this part of Anglesey. Then he came upon a further restriction to his progress; a slow-moving Austin 7 whose unhurried driver, despite incessant horn-sounding and the shouted curses and protestations of a furious police constable, obstinately refused to give way. Indeed, the driver, (a local man, known to Wynne Jones) appeared to be deliberately slowing down. Unaware of the urgency of the situation, the Austin's driver must have decided, in what seemed an act of bloody-mindedness, that the car behind him was not going to be allowed to overtake, come what may.

Eventually the policeman arrived at Cae Mawr, where fires were still burning and where Miss Jones' father was attempting to beat out some of the flames with a shovel. These attempts proved unsuccessful until the appearance of the Fire Service on the scene. Some thirty yards from the area of the main wreckage the body of the crashed aircraft's pilot was found draped across a wall. The man's body was in a mutilated condition and his clothes were on fire. The flames were quickly extinguished.

At Valley, the leader's unscheduled landing with his aircraft in a damaged condition and no explanation as to why his wingmen had disappeared could only mean one thing, as far as the RAF authorities were concerned: there had been an accident. At that moment they could only obtain, from information provided by the surviving pilot, an approximate crash location, somewhere in the northern part of Anglesey, close to the coast. But the RAF did not have to wait long for more precise information. Once the local police were told by Wynne Jones that two aircraft had crashed at Rhydwyn, details were immediately passed to Valley. The result was a flurry of messages sent from the airfield and soon the Admiralty, RNAS Anthorn, HMS *Illustrious* and the Netherlands Embassy, in London, knew of the crash of two Dutch Sea Furies and the death of their pilots. And so did their leader. What his feelings were upon being told that both his wingmen were dead, we can only imagine. Later, he visited the crash site and is recorded as having said to Christiana Jones, 'You're lucky to be alive', to which she replied, 'So are you'. Two years later the man's luck ran out. On 24 October 1955, by which time he had reached the rank of Lt. Commander, he was killed in a flying accident at the Dutch naval airbase of Valkenburg, near The Hague.

At Cae Mawr and Pen-y-Foel, the wreckage of the Sea Furies had to be protected from plunder by souvenir hunters and so a crash guard was installed. During the first night the guard was made up of policemen, whom Christiana Jones kindly provided with tea and refreshments to see them through their nocturnal vigil. On the following day, Wednesday the 20th, they were replaced by a military guard, who lived in tented accommodation at the site and remained there for over a week. The guard, according to Wynne Jones consisted of Royal Navy personnel, though on this point there is a difference of opinion between him and his sister, who maintains the men were Royal Marines. But whichever branch of the armed forces these men came from, they proved a magnetic attraction to many of the area's female populance, whose daily existence was much enlivened by this sudden infusion of highly desirable masculinity into their midst. As the old saying goes, 'It's an ill wind . . . '

If cordiality was an aspect of the guards' relationships with local girls the same could not be said of their attitude towards Wynne Jones. Before long he was in conflict with these uniformed sentinels of the crash site. He had moved the Sea Fury's wing from the front of his house because it was blocking access to his outbuildings, he claimed, and he had also tried to clear his farmyard of the debris that littered it. The instruction to 'Leave everything where it is' had been ignored and the farmer was duly admonished for his disobedience.

Despite the extreme disruption he was suffering, the loss of his livestock and damage to his property the farmer, who was also a keen gardener, maintained a sense of humour. Speaking to a neighbour who came to commiserate and see for himself the damage, he said, *'Edrycha ar y llanast yma – a mae o wedi difetha fy slots i yn lân!'*, ('Look at the mess here – and my shallots have been completely spoilt!'). His sister was not without a sense of humour either. When talking to the present author about the crash, she remarked that one of the buildings damaged by the aircraft was an outside toilet, or *tŷ bach* as it is often referred to in Welsh, (literally, the small house). The toilet had been completely demolished – 'and we only put a new seat in it a week previously', she said.

As can be imagined, news of the accident spread like wildfire through the local community and Wynne Jones' commiserating neighbour was far from being a lone individual. Many others were drawn to Pen-y-Foel and Cae Mawr to view the scene of the twin crashes. Amongst these onlookers was none other than the Llanfechell garage proprietor, Currie Hughes, to whom, it will be remembered, Christiana Jones had intended taking a wet battery that evening. Seizing her opportunity, she went up to Hughes and asked him if he would mind picking up the battery before he left. He would be glad to do so, he said, and so it was that Miss Jones succeeded in getting the battery charged after all.

* * *

The 'how and why' of a flying accident is, of course, a matter of great importance and requires careful investigation. In the case of the Dutch Sea Furies, the Navy set up a Board of Inquiry* which was to convene at RAF Valley on Friday, 22 May. The Board was made up of five members: two officers of Lt. Commander rank from RNAS Culham, (one of whom was an aviation specialist), a Surgeon Commander from RNAS

---

*The Board's papers and all subsequent Admiralty correspondence on the subject are in the Public Record Office, under the reference Adm 1/25017. HMS *Illustrious'* log for 19 May, 1953 is in Adm 53/135355.

Stretton, a Lt. Commander from the Royal Netherlands Navy and a Captain (who was a non-aviator) from RNAS Culham acting as the Board's President. As we shall see, the Inquiry proved to be inadequate in many ways and almost certainly came to the wrong conclusions.

Six witnesses were questioned: the Dutch Flight leader, Valley's Meteorological Officer and Senior Medical Officer, Wing Commander Cox, and two officers from HMS *Illustrious*, the Operations Officer and Meteorological Officer. First of the six to give evidence was the Flight leader. He was requested to give his version of events leading up to the crash, which he did, and was then asked about the height he had flown across Anglesey.

Q. Did you actually notice that you were at 900 feet?
A. Yes, I read it on my altimeter.
Q. How, where and when did you check your altimeter?
A. I set it to zero feet before taking off from HMS Illustrious.

The next two witnesses were from Valley – Wing Commander Cox, who gave evidence of his sighting of the aircraft shortly before they crashed, and the station's Meteorological Officer, a civilian by the name of Joseph Raybould, who provided the Board with details of local weather on the 19th. He was then questioned about the altimeter settings.

Q. If [the Flight leader] set his altimeter to zero on the deck of HMS Illustrious off Start Point at 1630 [hours] how would the changed barometric conditions affect his altimeter reading at 1800 [hours] at Valley?
A. The barometric change between Start Point (1630) and Valley (1800) is approximately eight millibars as judged from the relevant charts. The pressure at Valley being lower than at Start Point. This is equivalent to an altimeter change of 240 feet.
Q. Am I right in saying therefore that if his altimeter was reading 240 feet over Anglesey he would in fact have been

flying at approximately sea level?
A. Yes.

Raybould was followed by another meteorological officer, that of HMS *Illustrious*, for whom there was much more at stake in the outcome of the Inquiry than his RAF counterpart. He was the man who had briefed the Dutch pilot prior to the fatal flight. Asked by the Board to give an account of that briefing, he replied:

I stated that there would be thick cloud with rain and moderate to poor visibility over about the last two thirds of the route including destination. I mentioned in particular that high ground would be obscured by cloud and advised that a coastal route avoiding such high ground should be chosen. I added the suggestion that any part of the flight over land should be carried out above safety height. I was asked for cloud top and stated that it was probably in the region of 15,000 feet with main base at, so far as I can remember, 700 to 1,000 feet but with large stratus banks below, particularly over land. For diversion I stated that airfields in Southern England, i.e. south of the cloud area, would be suitable.

The questioning continued:

Q. Did you advise [the Flight leader] on the best way to get to Anthorn?
A. Only as I have already stated that the route over high ground should be avoided and that cloud base would be higher over the sea than the land.
Q. Did you at any time recommend that the best route . . . to follow might be over the sea at low level?
A. Yes, presuming that if [the Flight leader] found conditions over such a route to be poor, he would choose an alternative route.

Wreckage of Sea Fury *F-28 lies in a field a few yards from Cae Mawr farm, Rhydwyn.*
Photo: Crown copyright

The wreckage of Sea Fury *F-28 at Cae Mawr.*
Photo: Crown copyright

Lieutenant Hans Statius Muller of the Royal Netherlands Navy, killed in the crash of Sea Fury *F-28 at Cae Mawr farm.*
Photo: via Elisabeth Wegener Sleeswijk

Sea Fury *F-43 which survived the mid-air collision at Rhydwyn. This aircraft was eventually preserved at the Military Aviation Museum, Soesterberg, Holland.*
Photo: Military Aviation Museum, Soesterberg.

Cae Mawr, Rhydwyn, 26 May 1998. Left to right: Arthur Jones,
Christiana Jones, Elisabeth Wegener Sleeswijk, Roy Sloan.
Photo: Helga Danninger

Elisabeth Wegener Sleeswijk, widow of Lt. Hans Statius Muller, at the site
where her husband's Sea Fury crashed in May 1953.
Photo: Roy Sloan

Aviation enthusiast Arthur Evans (nearest the camera), who saw and attempted to photograph Vulcan XA909 *shortly before it crashed. Mr Evans is standing by the wreckage of* Gnat XR949, *which crashed near Bala in May 1964.*
Photo: via Arthur Evans

Avro Vulcan XA901, *sister-ship to* Vulcan XA909 *which crashed at Gwalchmai, Anglesey in July 1964.*
Photo: Map

The wreckage of Vulcan XA909 *lies burning in a field near Gwalchmai on 16 July 1964.*
Photo: via Hugh Williams

Beagle Basset XS783, *which crashed near Tŷ Croes on 5 July 1973.*
Photo: Map

A Hughes 269C *light helicopter similar to the one that crashed at Rhosgoch on 25 October 1979.*
Photo: Map

Westland Whirlwind XP349 of 'C' Flight, 22 Squadron, RAF Valley.
Photo: Manchester Evening News

The helipad from which **Hughes 269C** *helicopter G-BBIU took off in October 1979 and crashed into nearby power lines. Note the pylon close to the helipad.*
Photo: Roy Sloan

Gnat XR985 *which crashed at RAF Valley on 5 April 1965.*
Photo: via Arthur Evans

Wreckage of Gnat XR543 *being pulled from Maelog Lake, Rhosneigr. The aircraft crashed into the lake on 19 July, 1965.*
Photo: David Sutcliffe

The Wreckage of Gnat XS108 *loaded on to a lorry. This aircraft crashed at Valley on 22 April 1965 after being involved in a mid-air collision with* Gnat XR950 *near Caernarfon.*
Photo: via Arthur Evans

Flight Lieutenant Douglas Mee (left), the pilot of Gnat XR541 when it had a barrier engagement at RAF Mona on 7 February 1978. The photograph dates from the 1950s and shows the RAF Valley aerobatic team, of which F/Lt Mee was a member.

Photo: via Flight Lieutenant D. Mee

Gnat XR541 *after a barrier engagement, RAF Mona, 7 February 1978.*

Photo: via Flight Lieutenant D. Mee

Ruts caused by Gnat XR541, *RAF Mona, 7 February 1978.*
Photo: via Flight Lieutenant D. Mee

An aerial view of Gnat XR541's *barrier engagement at RAF Mona on 7 February 1978.*
Photo: via Flight Lieutenant D. Mee

Hawker Hunter F.6 XF384. One of two aircraft which crashed at the Silver Bay caravan park, Rhoscolyn after a mid-air collision on 10 August 1972. The other aircraft was Hunter F.6 XF387.

Photo: via Arthur Evans

Bae Hawk XX164, *which crashed moments after becoming airborne at RAF Valley on 13 February 1996.*

Photo: Map

Jodel D112 G-BHFF *following a ground accident at RAF Mona on 3 October, 1993. After an engine start without a pilot on board, the aircraft became a runaway and collided with the control tower.*
Photo: Eryl Crump

RAF Valley in the late 1950s.
Photo: via David J. Smith

RAF Mona, photographed in May 1960.
Photo: Crown copyright

Site of the former Saunders-Roe Factory and flying-boat base at Beaumaris, photographed in 1987.
Photo: Roy Sloan

RAF Bodorgan during the Second World War.
Photo: Crown copyright

After a few more questions on barometric pressure, during which the officer said that he agreed with his civilian colleague about the eight millibar difference in pressure between Start Point and Valley, he was allowed to stand down. However, this was far from being the end of the matter for him.

The Operations Officer of HMS *Illustrious* was next to give evidence, which centred upon the briefing given to the Dutch pilot:

Q. What was [the pilot's briefing]?
A. He was given a diversionary airfield at Shawbury and all the salient features of normal briefing were summarised on a photostatic copy which was given to the Pilot.
Q. Was he told at which height to fly?
A. No, but he was advised to fly at 6,000 feet. This was not intended to constitute an order.
Q. Do you mean by that, that you consider it is the Pilot's own responsibility to decide at what height to fly?
A. Yes.
Q. Why was he advised to fly at 6,000 feet?
A. My appreciation of the weather situation was that bad flying conditions would exist north of Shawbury. It was intended that advice concerning continuing the flight could have been obtained from [Shawbury].

For the Operations Officer, like *Illustrious'* Meteorological Officer, the evidence they gave at Valley did not bring their involvement in the investigation to a close. On the contrary, they made things worse for themselves and were deeper in trouble than before. Soon, the two men were to find themselves being hauled over the coals by the Admiralty.

Last of the six witnesses was Valley's SMO, Squadron Leader J.D. Crowlesmith, who said that he arrived at the scene of the accident at 6.45 p.m. and found both pilots dead. He listed their injuries, from which it was clear that neither the Cae Mawr or Pen-y-Foel crash was survivable.

The questioning of witnesses ended with the Dutch pilot being asked to give details of his Instrument Flying (IF) qualifications – an important point and one of great relevance to the Inquiry:

Q. What is your instrument rating?
A. White Card.
Q. Do you consider you have enough experience to qualify for your Green Instrument Rating?
A. Yes, but I have not had the opportunity.

This answer revealed his relative inexperience. A pilot who was not fully proficient but was capable of basic instrument flying held a White Card, whilst a more advanced pilot possessed a Green Card with a third category, the Master Green, reserved for pilots capable of instrument flying in any weather. In fact, the Dutch pilot had spent fifty hours in the (ground-based) Link trainer and forty-five hours actually flying in IF conditions. His two wingmen were even more inexperienced – the pilot of F-25 had logged fourteen hours of actual IF flying and the pilot of F-28 had fifteen hours – though, of course, this inexperience had no bearing upon the accident. It was only the leader who was flying on instruments. To maintain formation his wingmen would have had their eyes glued on the lead Sea Fury and nothing else. Even in good visibility formation flying demands total concentration, while in poor conditions it can become almost impossible or dangerous, as this particular accident was to prove.

The final statement in the transcript of the Board's proceedings reads: 'All log cards, Forms A.700 and relevant technical documents were inspected by the Board and found to be in order . . . No technical failure is suspected.' What, then, had gone wrong with the flight?

The Board, in submitting its findings to higher authority, in this case, Rear-Admiral L.E. Rebbeck, the Rear-Admiral Reserve Aircraft, said:

The position of the wreckage and also the state of the port wing tip of the aircraft which landed leads us to believe that he hit a solid and stationary object (possibly a wall or side of a house) in cloud with its port wing and tore away a large part of the tip [approximately eighteen inches] and about one third of the aileron. That the other two aircraft struck rising ground in parallel tracks without any contact with each other or the leader. This theory is substantiated by the fact that the leader's altimeter was reading about 240 feet high. This was established by the evidence of two separate met. officers and corroborated by the leader himself, who set it at zero on leaving Illustrious and had not altered it during flight.

But was this theory correct? On the very same day as the Board convened at RAF Valley, a local newspaper, the *Holyhead Chronicle* (22 May 1953) reported that, ' . . . the crash is believed to have been caused when the leader in the formation was in collision with the second aircraft, resulting in the second plane colliding with the third Sea Fury . . . ' Again, on that same day, the Commanding Officer (CO) of RNAS Anthorn was completing an Admiralty form (Form A.25 – Report on Aircraft Accident) in respect of the Sea Furies. In the report, two of Anthorn's officers, the Squadron Commander and Commander (Air) gave their views on the crash. First, the Squadron Commander:

In my opinion the accident occurred because of No.2 closing in on the leader of the formation too roughly and hit [*sic*] the leader's Port aileron and wing tip with his prop[eller]. No.2 then probably crossed underneath No.1 (which always gives the aircraft above an up lift) and consequently rammed No.3. No.2 and 3 came down together and hit the ground simultaneously in a practically horizontal position. All this happened in cloud.

Secondly, the Commander (Air):

It is considered that this accident was caused by an error of judgement on the part of an inexperienced pilot whilst endeavouring to keep formation in bad weather. It is probable that the No.2 of the Flight struck the leader from below and then became interlocked with No.3.

Anthorn's CO did not disagree with his fellow-officers: 'The cause of the accident was an error of judgement by an inexperienced pilot, a contributory cause being the weather conditions experienced en route.' There was, therefore, a complete difference between the Board of Inquiry's findings and the views of Anthorn's senior officers, the former attributing the crash to a ground collision and the latter to a mid-air collision. Clearly, both assessments could not be right. In the event, it was the Board's assessment which came to be regarded as incorrect – and not just incorrect but having serious shortcomings. Then the brickbats started to fly, the first coming from Rear-Admiral Rebbeck.

On 30 May he passed the Board's findings and minutes to the Navy's Flag Officer Air (Home), Vice-Admiral J. Eccles, at Lee-on-Solent with the observation that the flight briefing given aboard the *Illustrious* was revealed to be inadequate. Rebbeck made this claim because the Briefing Forms had omitted, 'Weather Information, Wind Speeds or Directions, Hazards on route, Safety Height', secondly, 'The height to fly was contrary to the Quadrantal height rules' and thirdly, 'The weather conditions were such that an Instrument Flight Brief was mandatory'. But the strongest criticism was reserved for the surviving pilot, upon whom the Rear-Admiral poured scorn. He wrote; 'The airmanship displayed by [the leader] during the flight was atrocious.' 'From his own evidence', Rebbeck continued, 'it is clear that he does not have the ability and judgement required by a Naval pilot and that he should not hold any British Instrument Grading.' Harsh words indeed.

For a few weeks Vice-Admiral Eccles pondered upon the Board's findings and came to the same conclusion as Rear-

Admiral Rebbeck: the findings were seriously flawed. 'While the opinion of the Board may well be correct', said Eccles, 'the recorded evidence is insufficient to show how it has been arrived at or why any other possible causes of the accident were not considered.' There was lack of evidence on, for example, whether or not the leader had collided with any solid or stationary object. 'Such an object would have been damaged by the aircraft', claimed Eccles. Furthermore, evidence was lacking on the IF category of the two pilots who were killed, R/T messages that passed between the aircraft and ship or shore stations, the contents of the Airmove signal made by *Illustrious* to RNAS Anthorn, and the height of the ground where the Sea Furies crashed. This, however, was not the end of the criticism:

No remarks are made on the pilot's statement . . . that he was flying at an indicated height of 900 feet which would, allowing for an error of 240 feet, still give him a margin of 150 feet over the high ground in Anglesey. Nor is any comment made on the briefing for the flight by H.M.S. ILLUSTRIOUS, which appears inadequate and, in some respects, incorrect. . . . '

Vice-Admiral Eccles wrote in the file, 'I have informed the Commanding Officer, R.N. Air Station Culham [where the Board's President was based] of my dissatisfaction with the inadequacy of the Board's enquiries.' Having told Culham of his concerns – which must have been greeted with dismay at the Air Station – Eccles also decided to take up some of his criticisms directly, on 24 June, with the captain of HMS *Illustrious*, Captain R.D. Watson. Watson was forced to defend the briefing given aboard his ship to the Dutch pilot. In a memo dated 23 July, he wrote:

' . . .[The leader] was ordered to fly to Anthorn via Shawbury. In view of the [limited] experience of the pilots with him, and his own instrument rating (White Card) he was told that he was not to lead his formation into I.F. conditions; this was qualified by instructions that should bad weather be met with, he was to contact Shawbury . . . for onward clearance. If he encountered I.F. conditions at any stage he was to return South where V.F.R. conditions were known to prevail and land at a suitable airfield . . . Since [the leader] had been ordered to remain in V.F.R. conditions no Instrument Flight Brief was given. . . . '

On the remaining points, Weather Briefing, Hazards on Route, Safety Height and Quadrantal Heights, Captain Watson was satisfied, he told Vice-Admiral Eccles, that his Operations Officer had briefed the Dutch pilot properly. And if Captain Watson was satisfied, so was Vice-Admiral Eccles. As far as he was concerned, the *Illustrious* was now exonerated from blame. He passed the file to the Admiralty in early August and wrote, 'No further action is intended regarding this accident.' If, by attempting to draw a line underneath the affair, the Vice-Admiral hoped to save some of *Illustrious'* officers (and himself!) from the potential embarrassment that continued investigation might bring, he was wrong. The Admiralty had other ideas. Captain Watson's memo gave a 'one-sided' version of events and had 'thrown little new light' on the accident, it was claimed. Instead of clarifying matters, the memo served, in the Admiralty's eyes, only to raise even more doubts about the findings of the Board of Inquiry. 'A sharp difference of opinion would appear to arise between Admiralty Branches and the Flag Officer . . . ', wrote an official. At that point, Vice-Admiral Eccles must have realised that the chances of the papers being quietly filed away and forgotten had disappeared.

Because of the 'difference of opinion' and apparent conflicts between points made by Captain Watson and answers given to the Board's questions, the Admiralty asked for further probings to take place. The possibility of ordering a fresh Inquiry had also been considered, the drawback being that so much time – nearly three months – had passed since the accident. The Admiralty seemed to have a genuine wish to be fair to all parties, and whilst there was general agreement that the surviving pilot was to blame, 'Without further investigation it is not possible to establish with certainty whether [he] was guilty of an error of judgment or of disobedience of orders.' The latter was the more serious charge. As for the *Illustrious*, there was 'no doubt whatsoever that [the ship] was gravely to blame also' but at the same time there was an acknowledgement by her accusers of 'the dangers of misunderstanding between people who speak different languages.' This was a recognition of the possibility that a pre-flight briefing given in English to a pilot who was not a native speaker of that language might have contributed to the confusions that subsequently arose.

There were a number of questions to which the Admiralty's brass hats wanted answers: whether the flight was correctly authorised, whether meteorological conditions were adequately considered by the officer responsible for authorisation, and whether clear and precise orders had been given as to the routes to be followed. The latter question was raised because of the 'Recommendation of different routes by the Operations Officer and Met Officer and no coordination being apparent.' There was also the extent of the Flight leader's knowledge and experience to be considered and whether this knowledge was correctly assessed. His statements to the Board of Inquiry indicated 'ignorance of the U.K. Altimeter Setting Procedure', and furthermore, 'he was allowed to take off without the correct altimeter setting for the region of departure.' The Admiralty also pointed out another example of laxness and inconsistency:

RAF Shawbury was given as a diversionary airfield in spite of the fact that the weather there was likely to be poor . . . The flight was allowed to proceed into weather where I.F. conditions were certain, whilst at the same time, according to ILLUSTRIOUS' letter [of 23 July] the [Flight's leader] was instructed not to enter I.F. conditions, although this fact was not brought out at the Board of Inquiry.

At the end of October Captain Watson was requested, for the second time, to submit a report on the flight briefing held aboard his ship on 19 May. The report was submitted to the Admiralty early in December. In his submission, the Captain said that he had held what was in effect a mini-inquiry, involving all the officers concerned, including the Dutch pilot. The original Board 'does not appear to have inquired very fully into the briefing' admitted the Captain, saying that his investigations would establish the full facts. Once again, he sought to reassure his superiors that all the correct procedures had been followed aboard the aircraft-carrier on the day of the accident. For instance, the Operations Officer approving the flight did so on the understanding that the pilot intended to follow the officer's briefing. The pilot, Captain Watson claimed, did not inform the Operations staff of his 'intention of trying to go round by the coastal route, under cloud', and his flight most certainly would not have been approved had he expressed this intention. With regard to the giving of 'clear and precise' route orders the reply to the Admiralty's question was that 'no direct order was given . . . to fly a definite route.' Captain Watson conceded that the use of the word 'ordered' in his 23 July memo was misleading, and that 'briefed' would have been a more accurate word.

On the question of the pilot's ability, 'It is considered that a correct assessment . . . was made.' The Dutch flyer was 'the Senior Pilot of an Operational Squadron; he had flown from the ship on previous occasions and in the U.K. generally since 1945 . . .'

A total of sixteen probing questions were answered in lengthy replies by Captain Watson, and the 'questionnaire', as he termed it, returned to the Admiralty through Vice-Admiral Eccles' office. Eccles had had a change of mind about the continuance of investigations into the crash and was now pressing for a re-opening of the Inquiry. He had become rather more critical of the *Illustrious* than previously: 'There seems to have been little liaison between "Operations" and "Met" ', and, 'It is not understood how a V.F.R. clearance was given when the weather forecast was for I.F.R. conditions in the Shawbury area and northwards.' A few days before Christmas the Vice-Admiral sent Captain Watson's completed 'questionnaire' to the Admiralty with a note neatly summarising the cause of the accident:

It is apparent that the briefing for this flight was not as clear as it should have been, nor was it entirely in accordance with the regulations. The facts can only be ascertained by a further enquiry and it is doubtful whether, even then, they will all be revealed owing to the lapse of time since the accident happened. It is, however, certain that had [the Flight leader] obeyed his instructions or even adhered to the elementary rules of airmanship the accident would not have occurred, despite the ambiguity of his briefing.

Like Rear-Admiral Rebbeck, Eccles was hostile to the surviving Dutch pilot, as was an Admiralty high-ranking officer who read the 'questionnaire'. He went even further in his condemnation: 'The error on the part of the leader was due partly to inadequate briefing but also to stupidity in taking a formation of inexperienced pilots through cloud close to the ground.' Yet more harsh words spoken against the unfortunate Dutchman.

As 1954 dawned, the affair of the Sea Furies continued to rumble on within Admiralty departments, with complaints being voiced about the failure to institute a fresh Inquiry, a move that 'would have prevented an already chilly trail from getting any colder.' This failure was blamed on the 'forwarding authorities', those lower down the chain of command but still with the power to convene a new Inquiry. There was also the not unimportant matter of the Admiralty's dealings with the Dutch Navy. Since the time of the Board of Inquiry the Dutch had been waiting patiently for the release of the Board's proceedings, as they were considering taking disciplinary action against the surviving pilot. Captain Van de Vlies Bik, the Naval Attaché at the Netherlands Embassy had asked for the proceedings during the autumn of 1953 and was duly sent a copy of the file on 29 October, though its usefulness to the Captain was limited. In a covering letter Bik was told by an official that, ' . . . as the Admiralty have not yet formed final conclusions about the accident, you may wish to defer your own decisions until I write to you again, which I hope will be quite soon.' In the event, 'quite soon' turned out to be February 1954.

Meanwhile, internal discussions within Admiralty departments continued. A memo from the Director of Navigation and Direction (DND) dated 16 January tells us of the Director's reservations on the matter of providing adequate evidence for the Dutch to prosecute the surviving pilot: 'It is doubtful whether the evidence at present available is sufficient to enable such action to be taken without a number of R.N. witnesses being called by the Dutch. In D.N.D.'s opinion a gross injustice would be done if [the pilot] was to be court martialled and the ILLUSTRIOUS allowed to go scot free.'

But at some stage the protracted deliberations and flow of Admiralty memos had to stop. The case had already lasted for seven months. To resolve the situation, there were two options: either to re-open the Inquiry 'and get the whole truth' or to wind up the affair as it stood. The DND, 'influenced by the staleness of the evidence . . . and the amount of time which had already been wasted on this matter' chose, with some reluctance, the second option. Furthermore, the Director was extremely annoyed about what had happened since the accident: ' . . . the whole conduct of this inquiry has been most unsatisfactory', he wrote, and 'the prestige of the R.N. has suffered on this account in the eyes of the Dutch.'

The DND's colleagues, such as the Director of Air Warfare and the Director of Air Organisation and Training, agreed with him that the matter should be closed. At the beginning of February 1954 Vice-Admiral Eccles was told, by letter, of the

Admiralty's decision. The letter was written by a member of the Legal Deparment in that curious and somewhat excessively formal style adopted in correspondence of this nature: 'I am commanded by My Lords Commissioners of the Admiralty', the official wrote, 'to inform you that they agree with [your] views . . . but it is with reluctance that they have decided not to order the convening of a new Board of Inquiry'. To have had a reasonable chance of getting at the truth, a second Board should have been convened immediately the deficiencies of the first became apparent.

The *Illustrious*, however, still remained under fire. There was to be an overhaul of the ship's 'extremely poor' pre-flight briefing organisation, plus a reprimand for the Operations Officer and Met Officer, who were accused of being 'gravely to blame for the inadequate and confusing briefing' given to the Dutch pilot. Because of their negligence the two officers had incurred 'My Lords' displeasure.' 'Accordingly', said an official, 'I am to request that you [Vice-Admiral Eccles] convey to [the two officers] an expression of My Lords' displeasure.' Such was the etiquette of Naval top brass in giving the officers a dressing-down.

On 11 February Captain Van de Vlies Bik was told that the Admiralty had 'completed further enquiries into the accident' and, as far as the inadequate briefing given aboard *Illustrious* was concerned, 'disciplinary action other than by Court Martial is being taken against those responsible.' The Dutch Flight's leader was criticised also, but not surprisingly, gone were the scathing comments of senior officers. Their previously unrestrained remarks had been considerably toned down:

'. . . the [leader] was also at fault in entering I.F. conditions under the prevailing circumstances though this may have been no more than an error of judgement. (We [the Admiralty] do not consider an error of judgement to be a disciplinary offence and we distinguish it most carefully from negligence).

There is little doubt that if the pilot concerned was British, he would have faced a court martial, and if found guilty, his flying career with the Navy would have ended.

If the findings of the original Board of Inquiry were so unsatisfactory as to be rejected, can we, without the benefit of a second (and more thorough) Inquiry, be sure of what happened to the Sea Furies during the last two minutes of their flight across Anglesey? While there can be no absolute certainty about it, of course, the theory put forward by the Squadron Commander at RNAS Anthorn seems perfectly plausible – that the No.2 closed in on the leader 'too roughly', clipped the leader's port wing and then collided with No.3.

Of one fact, however, we can be certain: that between 5.50 p.m. and 5.55 p.m. the three-ship formation was flying on a northerly heading beneath the low cloudbase, as witnessed by Wing Commander Cox, who at that time was driving his car on the A5 road near Valley. About two minutes after this sighting, when the aircraft were approaching the cloud-obscured Carmel Head and Rhydwyn area, the leader could see that the low-lying ground, flashing by only a couple of hundred feet beneath the speeding Sea Furies, was rapidly giving way to rising ground which disappeared into the cloudbase. The leader knew that he had to climb forthwith, but did so with an altimeter, it will be remembered, that was giving a false reading of 240 feet below the actual height flown. Then, as altitude was gained and clouds closed in around the three aircraft, the inexperienced No.2, aware that he *had* to maintain visual contact with the lead Sea Fury in these difficult conditions, moved in closer so as not to lose that vital contact but he did so 'too roughly', resulting in the mid-air collision which brought disaster to the Flight.

The height of the ground where the two wingmen's aircraft impacted is 460 feet (140 metres). Furrows were created at the initial point of impact of both aircraft, leading to a wreckage trail extending for over a quarter of a mile. This pattern of wreckage distribution suggests that the Sea Furies were in a relatively level position when they struck the ground and there had not been time after the mid-air collision for the subsequent loss of control to develop into a terminal dive. Had this been the case, then instead of furrows there would be craters, and most of the wreckage would either be inside the craters or concentrated around their rims. In other words, the ground collision followed on almost immediately from the mid-air collision. This suggests, therefore, that the formation was flying at an altitude that was only slightly (another twenty or thirty feet perhaps) above the ground which they hit. Now, the leader's altimeter was, for reasons already described, wrongly indicating an additional 240 feet of height – height that simply was not there. Add that 240 feet to the 460 – 480 feet at which the aircraft were actually flying, and a figure of between 700 feet and 720 feet is arrived at. This would have been the height at which the leader (mistakenly) thought he was. Having looked, as he later claimed, at his map and noted there were hills at 500 feet, he must have felt confident that he had sufficient altitude to clear this ground, and if his no.2 had not made the fatal misjudgement then the Flight would probably have scraped (almost literally so) over the ground where Pen-y-Foel and Cae Mawr farms are located.

As regards the leader's statement that after looking at his map he climbed, 'in cloud to 900 or 1,000 feet, intending to cross Anglesey', it is impossible to reconcile this claim with the fact of Wing Commander Cox's sighting of the Sea Furies at 200 feet. This sighting was by a totally reliable witness and belies the Dutch pilot's claim. In all likelihood, the formation crossed the island in visual conditions, flying underneath the low cloudbase until such time as the leader was forced to climb into cloud because of rising ground.

But whatever the accuracy of this analysis of the immediate cause of the accident, there were also three contributary factors, summarised in an Admiralty memo dated 25 August 1953:

(a) That the division of Sea Furies was allowed to take off on this flight into weather conditions where low visibility was certain, and when at least two of the pilots had very limited experience.

(b) That the decision for the flight to proceed having been taken, both the general and meteorological briefing were confusing, imprecise, and incomplete.

(c) That the leader pilot continued his flight in the weather conditions prevailing instead of returning to an alternative airfield to the South where clear weather was known to exist.

Assuming the Flight had cleared the rising ground at Rhydwyn (by only a few feet) and had then actually succeeded in reaching RNAS Anthorn, there would have been the further problem, previously mentioned, of the airfield's closure for flying at 6.00 p.m. that day. To make matters worse, although the Airmove signal, marked 'Operational Immediate' had been sent at 4.45 p.m. from HMS *Illustrious* to Anthorn (with a copy to RAF Shawbury), giving information that the Sea Furies were on their way, this signal turned out to be anything but 'Immediate'. For some reason it was delayed and was not received at Anthorn until 6.20 p.m., five minutes *after* the receipt of a signal that the aircraft were missing and half an hour after they had crashed. 'It is possible, then', said an Admiralty official, 'that even had the three Dutch officers completed the flight, the airfield at their destination would have been closed.' For the official it was another 'disturbing fact' to add to an already long list arising from 'this deplorable accident and inadequate investigation.'

If the 'mid-air collision' theory was the one which found most favour with the British, it was also accepted by the Dutch. They too had decided to reject the findings of the Board of Inquiry. A letter dated October 1967, written by the Historical Section of the Netherlands Navy to an aviation historian from Gwynedd, (not the author), said: 'On 19th May 1953 the Sea Furies F25 and F28 crashed near Rhydwyn in North Wales after a collision in the air.' In 1999 the author received a similar reply in response to his enquiry: 'The planes with the registration numbers F-25, F-28 and F-43 . . . collided with each other in a dense sheet of clouds.'

As mentioned already, Sea Fury F-43 which the leader flew, was only slightly damaged in the accident and after having a new wing fitted it went back into service with the Dutch Navy. At the end of its useful life the aircraft was withdrawn from use and was destined for preservation in the Aviodome Museum at Schiphol Airport, Amsterdam. Eventually, because of continued expansion, the Aviodome exhausted all its display space and it was decided to move F-43 to the Military Aviation Museum at Soesterberg. Like the Aviodome, this museum was also expanding and by the 1990s had reached the limits of the space that could be utilised. This resulted in the Sea Fury being put into storage and at the time of writing (1999) it remained in storage and was not available for public viewing.

The Admiralty's final act arising out of the 'inadequate investigation' of the Anglesey accident was to issue a general warning to the Navy's various commands, both home and abroad, about the need to maintain standards. A signal dated 10 February 1954 reads:

Their Lordships have been disturbed by the incompleteness of the reports of some recent Boards of Inquiry into aircraft accidents. The Boards have tended to occupy themselves with comparatively unimportant detail and have not devoted sufficient attention to fundamental principles and regulations . . . [It is requested] that every effort should be made to set high standards for such reports.

Thus was the 'unhappy affair' of the Dutch Sea Furies and their loss brought to an end.

* * *

At Cae Mawr farm and the locality of Rhydwyn generally, no-one had the slightest inkling of the shortcomings of the Board of Inquiry or of the Admiralty's subsequent and prolonged review of the evidence. Such matters were entirely confidential, of course. Decades passed before Christiana Jones and her nephew, Arthur, came to know the truth. As far as they were concerned, the story had ended with the clearance of wreckage from their land.

It was during this clearance process that a watch belonging to the pilot of Sea Fury F-28 was discovered in a hedge at Cae Mawr and then returned to the man's widow in Holland. Concealed within the hedge was another item also – the pilot's cap badge but nearly half a century would pass before this article was returned to his widow. Many years after the accident, Christiana Jones' father came across the badge, and his daughter mounted it on a circular piece of cardboard decorated with sea shells, the whole protected from dust by a glass cover. It remained in her possession until 1981, when, upon first meeting the author, she passed it to him and in whose keeping it would remain for the next seventeen years.

After the removal of wreckage and the making good of damage at Cae Mawr and Pen-y-Foel, life returned to normal, though, as one would expect, the shocking events of that mist-shrouded and dramatic May afternoon remained a major topic of conversation long afterwards. However, the relentless passage of time dimmed the immediacy of the story and as the weeks turned into months and the months into years and the years into decades, the crash of the Sea Furies became nothing more than another part of local history. Then, forty-two years later, during the summer of 1995, the Clerk of the Garn and District Community Council (which encompassed the area of Rhydwyn) received a letter from a Dutch woman by the name of Elisabeth Wegener Sleeswijk, living in the Swiss city of Zürich. Frau Wegener Sleeswijk was enquiring about the Rhydwyn crash. She wanted to know all about the event – its precise location, was it possible to visit the site, any descriptive press cuttings etc. – but she did not provide an explanation as to why this information was required, although it was clear that she had considerable personal interest in the subject.

Eventually her letter landed on the author's desk. He, in collaboration with Christiana Jones, then entered into correspondence with the enquirer, who revealed that she had been married to the pilot killed in the Sea Fury (F-28) which crashed at Cae Mawr. His name was Hans Statius Muller. The two had met at the end of the Second World War and it was a case of 'love at first sight', said Frau Wegener Sleeswijk. They were espoused soon afterwards. In 1951 Elisabeth accompanied her young husband to the United States, where he undertook flying training at the Naval Air Station, Pensacola, in Florida. Upon the couple's return to the Netherlands they looked forward to creating a happy, secure future for themselves and their two children, but it was all taken away from them by the cruel and tragic events at Cae Mawr. The rainbow of their hopes had simply been swallowed up in the mists swirling around the Anglesey farm.

Lieutenant Statius Muller's widow had been given surprisingly few details of the crash and its causes, except unofficially and in confidence by a senior officer in the Dutch Navy, who said to her that the Sea Furies were flying too low because of an incorrect altimeter setting, though as we have seen, this was only part of a much more complicated story. The newly-widowed Dutch woman understood little of the technicalities of aviation but she fully understood that, regardless of how the aircraft was brought down, the loss which resulted had altered the shape of her life forever. At that time she and her husband were living, with their children, in an attic, which they occupied whilst waiting for a house to be provided for them by the Dutch Navy. Unfortunately, following the accident there was no possibility of the family being given a house. As a widow, Elisabeth Wegener Sleeswijk no longer qualified for this type of accommodation. The Naval authorities were not without compassion, however, and declared that they were willing to rent a flat for her, provided she found one through her own efforts. It was like looking for a needle in a haystack, she recalled.

She was also desperately short of money and was forced to take a part-time job to help make ends meet and rear her now-fatherless children. The outlook seemed bleak. Then she met a young Swiss student who fell in love with her and asked her to marry him, which she did. The couple moved to Switzerland. There, Elisabeth strove, she said, 'to be a good Swiss wife and leave everything behind that had been, including the memory of my time with Hans.' In 1995 she and her second husband separated and she found herself thinking more and more of the long-dead pilot who had been her first marriage partner. She realised that, in spite of all the years that had passed, she had not properly come to terms with her loss.

This resulted in such a strong urge to visit the place where her aviator husband died that she actually began to formulate a plan to travel to Anglesey, hence her exploratory letter to the Garn and District Community Council. The author, when he became involved, indicated that both he and Miss Christiana Jones were willing to assist as much as possible and travel details were in the process of being finalised at the end of 1995 when contact was discontinued from the Swiss side mainly because Frau Wegener Sleeswijk could not find a suitable date when her two daughters would be free to travel with her, and she did not wish to travel alone. Silence followed and by 1998 the author was convinced nothing more would be heard and that the matter was concluded. Then, in early May of that year he received a letter from Zürich explaining that on 23 May Frau Wegener Sleeswijk was travelling to Edinburgh to meet a female friend, Helga Danninger, also from Zürich, who was in the Scottish capital on business. The two friends planned to spend some time in the UK, including a visit to Anglesey if the author and Miss Jones were in agreement with the plan. Both were and so a date was set for the visit: Tuesday, 26 May, which, the author later discovered was the forty-fifth anniversary of Lt. Statius Muller's funeral. On that day in 1953 his body, having been taken back to Holland, was cremated and his ashes scattered from an aircraft flying above the English Channel.

Thus, forty-five years later, to the month, five people – Elisabeth Wegener Sleeswijk (looking much younger than her sixty-nine years), her friend, Helga Danninger, the author, Miss Christiana Jones (by then in her eighties and not in the best of health) and her nephew Arthur Jones (the previously mentioned eleven-year old boy and now a mature man in his mid-fifties) met at Cae Mawr. Plainly, it was an emotional time for Frau Wegener Sleeswijk. She had been given her husband's cap badge after its safekeeping by the author for seventeen years and there was also the upsetting news of a flying accident in Snowdonia a few days previously, on 23 May. Two young men were killed in a light aircraft (Cessna 150 G-BIIJ) which became lost in bad weather and flew into cloud-obscured high ground – similar circumstances to those in which the two Dutchmen had lost their lives in 1953 – a similarity which did not escape the attention of the Swiss visitor. Particularly poignant for her was the fact that the Cessna's pilot had left behind a wife and two small children – children who were now fatherless, just as hers were in 1953. She thought that for an accident of this type to occur at the very time of her visit to Anglesey (on Tuesday the 26th unsuccessful attempts were being made to recover the Cessna's wreckage) was a remarkable coincidence and one which, for her, was of much significance.

At Cae Mawr she and her friend were treated to a typical Welsh *croeso* (welcome) and there was much *hwyl* (animated, light-hearted conversation) but there was a deeply serious side to the visit also. Indeed, it was the main reason why the 700-mile journey from Switzerland to North Wales had been embarked upon: to say a final goodbye to a long-dead husband at the actual spot where he had lost his life. Braving a cold and unseasonal northerly wind, the group – minus Miss Jones, who had to remain indoors because of her health – set off to visit the crash sites at Pen-y-Foel and Cae Mawr. Many photographs were taken (some of which are reproduced here) and at the location where the doomed aircraft first made contact with the ground Elisabeth Wegener Sleeswijk asked if she could be allowed a brief period of privacy. The others withdrew out of sight and earshot, leaving her alone with her thoughts and feelings. This was clearly the culmination of her journey. A few minutes later she rejoined the group, her pilgrimage to Anglesey satisfactorily concluded. She had achieved what she set out to achieve.

- 13 -

Escape from a Vulcan Bomber

On a July day in 1964 three men – an aviation enthusiast, a farmer and an RAF pilot – none of whom knew of the existence of the others, all experienced loss of one kind: the first lost a photographic opportunity, the second lost the use of a field, albeit temporarily while the third, through no fault of his own, lost his aircraft. And as the reader will have gathered, the circumstances of the losses are interconnected.

The Aviation Enthusiast
On Thursday the 16th aviation enthusiast Arthur Evans decided to go for a walk along the beach at Dinas Dinlle, close to the disused wartime airfield of RAF Llandwrog, a few miles south of Caernarfon. Whilst on the beach, Evans' attention was drawn skywards by the sound of an approaching jet aircraft. Looking up, he saw the distinctive and unmistakable delta-winged shape of an Avro Vulcan. Interestingly, the V-bomber was accompanied by another aircraft, a diminuitive Gnat which the onlooker correctly guessed was from RAF Valley. To his eye, the second machine looked even smaller when close to the huge jet.

Arthur Evans had his 35 m.m. camera with him and as the two aircraft, one as large as the other was tiny, flew overhead, Evans thought of taking a photograph but then hesitated, knowing that his camera lacked a telephoto lens to make the subject fill the frame and therefore create a more interesting image. As it was, he feared that any shot he would take would be unrewardingly dull, showing nothing more than a wide expanse of sky with the Gnat and the Vulcan as indistinct dots.

Feeling that his efforts would merely waste film, the flying buff held back from pushing the shutter release button, and as the jets quickly receded into the distance, so did the opportunity to record their passage. If, as the old saying goes, time and tide wait for no man, then fast-moving jet aircraft most certainly do not. When indecision was overcome and the camera button finally pushed, it was too late – the V-bomber was, as feared, only a blurred dot on the resultant photograph, while the Gnat was invisible except with the aid of a magnifying glass.Thus was lost an unique picture-taking opportunity. Arthur Evans watched the jets disappear towards Anglesey before continuing with his walk. Later, when he came to know the full story of the two aircraft and the critical condition one of them was in, he regretted wasting those few seconds when he had a reasonable chance of obtaining a photograph.

But then, how could he, as someone who just happened by chance to witness the Vulcan's flight, have possibly known anything of the truth beforehand? He was, at that stage, as unaware of the crisis surrounding the bomber as was the second person featured in this story . . .

The Farmer

Farmer Hugh Williams, a tall, distinguished-looking man with an urbane manner, who could easily have passed for a top civil servant or lawyer, earned his living through the husbandry of Treddolphin Farm near the village of Gwalchmai.

On the afternoon of the 16th, after he and his wife had eaten their lunch, they went to one of the farm's outbuildings to dose some ewes with medicine. Most country dwellers are familiar with that unique brand of animal stupidity which is ovine and Hugh Williams' flock was no exception. Nevertheless the farmer, with his wife's assistance, was making steady progress when their work was brought to an abrupt and frightening halt. Suddenly, the incessant bleating of the sheep, which until then had filled the couple's ears, was drowned by the thunderclap of an explosion close by.

Full of trepidation, the pair ran out of the building and were shocked by the sight that met their eyes; a field near to their farmhouse was littered from one end to another with burning, smoking wreckage. Hugh Williams quickly realised that an aircraft had crashed. Naturally enough, his instinctive reaction was to go to the assistance of any possible survivors and so he rushed to the field and began searching through the debris. He searched in vain, however. Not a single survivor could the farmer locate and never would, because of one simple fact; there was not a soul on board the Vulcan – for that was the aircraft – when it crashed. All the crew had baled out, including the third and most central of the three men portrayed in this brief narrative . . .

The RAF Pilot
Earlier that day Flight Lieutenant Mike Smith of 101 Squadron had taken off, with his four-man crew, in Vulcan XA909 from the squadron's base at RAF Waddington in Lincolnshire. The flight began as a routine training exercise but ended in a far from routine manner.

Having flown to the Scottish airport of Prestwick, the Vulcan was returning south, cruising at an altitude of 43,000 feet over Cardigan Bay when the uneventful nature of the flight came to a violent end after a bearing in the no.4 engine fractured. This caused an explosive disintegration of the low-pressure turbine disc, sending fragments of the disc and its casing into the neighbouring power plant and puncturing the airframe at many points. Not only had two engines been lost – a serious enough setback in itself – but there were control difficulties to contend with, in addition.

Smith reacted by sending out a Mayday signal and closing the throttles of the functioning engines to idle speed in order to initiate a descent but, as Smith suspected harm had been done to the wing surfaces, he did not extend the airbrakes. Soon the aircraft was intercepted by one of Valley's Gnats, whose pilot provided a great deal of assistance by reporting on the visible damage and, in particular, by calling out the V-bomber's airspeed. The three airspeed indicators in the Vulcan were all giving different readings as the pitot static system had been disabled by fragments from the failed engine. Let Flight Lieutenant Smith describe the emergency situation he faced;

We continued our descent all the way from 43,000 feet to about 3,000 feet. On levelling out I applied power to the two good engines for the first time [since the explosion] while the Gnat was checking our speed. Up to that point, while gliding down with the engines at idle, I had been using the secondary effect of applying rudder – first yaw, second roll – to bank the aircraft because the ailerons had failed. It then became apparent that when also using rudder to correct the yaw caused by the asymmetric power there was barely enough left to be able to control the bank angle. At this point [when the two aircraft were heading towards Valley] the Gnat told us that our speed was around 200 knots and I realised that I would have insufficient rudder to meet both the yaw and the roll requirements at landing speed.

Smith had initially hoped to land at Valley but once it became clear that there would be insufficient control available to do this safely an orderly abandonment became the only option. One additional factor preyed heavily on his mind; the Vulcan's inadequate escape system. Of the five crew only the pilot and co-pilot enjoyed the benefit of ejection seats, while the remaining three, who sat in a windowless compartment behind the cockpit, had only conventional parachutes. Escape for them was not easy except in the most favourable circumstances, and even then there was a problem if the undercarriage was down. Once the Vulcan's wheels were lowered, the nosewheel obstructed the rear crew's escape hatch and abandonment, though theoretically possible, was, in practical terms quite hazardous. The other option that Smith could have considered, that of attempting an approach to land and deciding at a late stage to abandon if things went wrong was, for him, out of the question.

The pilot's next step was to set up a practise bale out run at 3,000 feet – judged to be the optimum height for abandoning the aircraft – and he briefed the crew that he was going to fly seawards and that everyone was to bale out when the aircraft crossed the Anglesey coastline. This would ensure that wreckage would not fall on any of the dwellings Smith could see dotting the island's sunny landscape below him. It would also give the crew the chance of a soft landing in the sea, where they would rapidly be picked up by the rescue helicopters, which were already airborne. This plan was soon cast aside, however, when the Navigator (Radar) discovered, as he was preparing the escape hatch for abandonment, what appeared to be a ripcord handle that had become dislodged from his dinghy pack. Unbeknown to the rear crew, a modification had been carried out on their dinghy packs to replace the activating lanyard with a ripcord type D-ring, in order to make dinghy inflation simpler. The Navigator, unsure of the mysterious D-ring's purpose, and unwilling to risk it snagging as he slid down the exit hatch, thus caused the plan to jump into the sea to be modified.

Smith then decided that the only practical course of action was to get the crew to bale out just before they reached the coast so that they would parachute onto dry land and allow the aircraft to crash into the sea, but this plan, like the previous one, did not quite work out either. As speed was being reduced in the final turn onto the escape heading, maintaining control of the V-bomber became difficult and in the end Flight Lieutenant Smith gave the order to bale out earlier than intended and the aircraft never reached the sea.

First to exit was the Navigator (Radar), Flight Lieutenant A.R. Fraser, followed by the Navigator (Plotter), Flight Lieutenant A.W. Houghton, and finally the Air Electronics Officer, Flying Officer D.M. Evans. All managed to get safely through the escape hatch in the well of the Vulcan because of two important factors: first, the bomber was flying straight and level, and secondly, there was ample time to prepare for the jump. Without these factors, the outcome could have been very different – something which the crew were only too aware of. Additionally, of course, the presence of the Gnat was an enormous boon, with the pilot keeping a watchful eye on the progress of the three crewmen as their parachutes blossomed into life-saving canopies.

Meanwhile, Smith and his co-pilot, Flying Officer G. Woods, after observing their three colleagues slide out through the escape hatch, hastened to bring about their own departure from the aircraft. As mentioned previously, they had ejection seats to speed them (literally) on their way but first the cockpit canopy had to be jettisoned. This could be achieved either automatically or manually, the pilot's choice being the latter method. In a moment the canopy was gone, producing a marked nose-up change of trim and severe buffeting. At this time the Vulcan was at 3,200 feet, flying at a speed of 220 knots, with the ever-vigilant Gnat pilot providing a reassuring presence to ease the burden on Mike Smith. Then the co-pilot fired his ejection seat and was catapulted from the aircraft. His seat operated perfectly and he later made a safe landing.

Last to go, as befitted his senior position was Flight Lieutenant Smith. But when he pulled the firing lanyard of his seat it seemed to him that nothing happened. For one heart – stopping instant he thought the seat had failed! Thus, with the face blind down, the pilot, following advice given during training, butted his head against the blind and tugged harder on the lanyard. To his immense relief the seat then fired. Looking back on this traumatic experience, it became clear to him that the failure of the seat was apparent rather than real. Writing in 1995, he explained;

I am now certain that my seat firing sequence initiated correctly at the first pull of the face blind. In the excitement I had forgotten that there was a one second delay built into the sequence to allow for automatic jettisoning of the canopy. We had elected to jettison it manually but the one second delay still occurred.

With his life at stake, that small interval of time – one second – felt like an eternity to Mike Smith. In fact, less than a minute later he was hanging from the straps of his parachute, watching the once-mighty Vulcan descending in an ever-steepening dive to its final destiny; complete destruction in a massive ball of flame.

Smith then turned his attention towards the ground, which was rapidly getting close. Having been on two parachute training courses and having done six jumps, he felt confident that he would be able to make a good landing but at the critical moment he braced himself incorrectly with the result that the touchdown was hard enough to daze him, though he quickly recovered his senses.

All of the five crew, believed to be the first to have successfully escaped from a Vulcan, landed in the vicinity of Gwalchmai and thanks to Valley's SAR helicopters and an ambulance from RAF Mona, the five were soon in the Station Sick Quarters (SSQ) at Valley, receiving medical attention.

For Mike Smith , however, the short period between ejecting and being helped into Valley's SSQ was full of anxiety because he did not know what had become of his colleagues. When he was safely aboard the SAR helicopter he asked a crewman, 'How many parachutes?' 'One', was the reply, much to the rescued pilot's dismay. Of course, there was plenty of opportunity for a misunderstanding to arise – the Whirlwind helicopter was very noisy and it was possible that both Smith and the crewman might have misheard each other. Equally, it could be that the crewman did, in fact, see only one parachute (probably the co-pilot's) and was uninformed that the three rear crew had been picked up by an ambulance from RAF Mona. This vehicle had set off in pursuit of the men as soon as their descending parachutes were seen and at the very moment Mike

Smith was being rescued, the ambulance was already speeding towards Valley. Unaware of this fact, Smith was convinced that he had just lost three good friends – and possibly because of his own decision making – but upon arrival at the SSQ, his worries ended. 'The relief', he said, 'when I saw [the crew] laughing at me as I was helped into the sick bay at Valley was enormous.'

The worst injury was to the Navigator (Radar), who broke his leg upon landing. His two other colleagues, the Navigator (Plotter) and Air Electronics Officer emerged from the incident with nothing worse than a few minor cuts. Both of the pilots had bruised backs – the most frequent type of injury arising out of ejection – but nevertheless it was a small price to pay for survival. Mike Smith's back continued to be painful for some time after the accident, necessitating a lengthy period of recovery before he was able to resume his flying duties.

Although he had suffered the loss of his aircraft, and Hugh Williams the loss of his field and Arthur Evans the loss of a good photograph, the worst loss of all – loss of life – had mercifully been avoided. Flight Lieutenant Smith and his fellow survivors enjoyed many reunions in subsequent years to celebrate that fact and toast the Fates which had been so kind to them in their hour of extreme peril on that July day in 1964.

14

Avtur instead of Avgas

One of the privileges of being a senior RAF officer is that when you have to travel on offical business you are afforded the luxury of personal air transport. If your destination is an airfield or has one close to it, then no frustrating drive on overcrowded roads for you, no submitting to the tender mercies of railway companies, no mixing with the common herd. Instead, an aerial carriage is provided, courtesy of the taxpayer, entirely for your convenience, to take you speedily and efficiently to your journey's end. For those who possess it, high status always confers exclusiveness.

Such was the case at RAF Valley on Thursday, 5 July 1973, when the Station Commander, an officer of Group Captain rank, had to travel to the headquarters of No.23 Group, located at RAF Linton-on-Ouse, in Yorkshire. At 11.42 a.m. Beagle Basset XS783 of No.26 Communications Squadron, RAF Wyton, Bedfordshire, landed at Valley to fly the Station Commander to Linton. On board the aircraft was the usual two-man crew: pilot and navigator, the former a Squadron Leader, the latter a Flight Lieutenant. Upon arrival at the station's Transit Aircraft Servicing Flight (TASF), the pilot requested that his machine's fuel tanks be replenished. The NCO in charge of the duty shift telephoned for an AVGAS bowser but, fatefully, asked for an AVTUR bowser in addition, because the Flight also had a visiting jet aircraft, a Jet Provost, to refuel that morning.

The difference between the two fuels – AVGAS and AVTUR – is not only crucial to aviation operations generally but is also the main point upon which the present narrative hinges. AVGAS is, essentially, high grade petrol used in piston-engined flying while the less volatile, paraffin-based AVTUR is a jet fuel. All those who work with aircraft should know this fundamental and very important difference, for obvious reasons of flight safety.

At 12.15 p.m. the duty NCO at TASF went to lunch, informing one of his airmen that two bowsers would be arriving. The NCO detailed the airman to refuel the Basset first, which, because it was to carry the Station Commander, had priority over the Jet Provost. What happened next is not entirely clear because of conflicting evidence, but whatever the nature of the confusion at TASF that lunchtime, we can be certain of two facts: first, both an AVGAS and AVTUR bowser were present as requested, and secondly, the airman given the job of refuelling the piston-engined Basset did so with the wrong fuel. He put AVTUR instead of AVGAS into the aircraft's tanks. It was a mistake which was to cost the erring refueller his RAF career and the Basset navigator his life.

The airman's mistake was also a rare one. So much so that only two other 'wrong fuel' instances are on the RAF Inspectorate of Flight Safety's database, which goes back to 1971.* These incidents, involving a Jet Provost, in 1978, and a Pembroke, in 1984, were attributed to human error, though fortunately the mistakes were identified before the aircraft in question took off.

As far as the error at Valley is concerned, regardless of any administrative mix-up in the TASF office and the correctness or otherwise of the instructions given to the airman, when he came to perform the actual physical task of refuelling the Basset, he should have known, without taking heed of any other consideration, that the right fuel for the aircraft was AVGAS. Furthermore, the AVGAS bowser was clearly marked as such. In

*Perhaps there should also be a third instance if the *Daily Post* (Welsh edition, 30 January, 1974, p.3) is correct in its reporting of the subsequent court martial of the airman at TASF. 'In reply to Ieuan Redvers Jones [the accused's solicitor] he [the NCO in charge of TASF] agreed that another aircraft, a Bell helicopter, had been refuelled with the wrong fuel on the same morning. Fortunately in that case it was found out.' Redvers Jones's comment on TASF, 'There was no supervision here' seems almost mild.

fact, both bowsers would have had the fuel type they contained conspiciously written in large letters on the vehicle's bodywork for all to see.

This was a very important point and bowser markings formed a major part of the subsequent inquiry into the loss of the Basset. To quote from the accident report;

> The need for improved refueller markings has been examined by the Engineering Staff at MoD(AFD). RAF refuelling procedures and the requirements for fuel grade markings were thoroughly overhauled and modernised during 1972 after extensive study and consultation which brought in all interested parties and relevant experience. They have examined the circumstances of this accident [to XS783] and are of the opinion that it does not point to a weakness in the identification markings. This tragic accident was caused by unavoidable human error, together with poor organisation and supervision.

But however visible the Valley bowser's markings, the hapless airman failed to take note of these indications of content. As a result, the Basset's safety was seriously compromised by the mismanaged refuelling operation though none of the people about to fly in the aircraft knew this. Such are the risks of flying.

The Station Commander's wife was supposed to accompany him on the flight to Linton, but she suffered from angina and had experienced an attack earlier that day sufficient to deter her from travelling. At 1.40 p.m. the Group Captain arrived at TASF without his spouse and boarded the waiting machine, which was flown by the same two-man crew as before.

After a normal engine start and checks, the Basset began to taxi and reached the runway without any hint of trouble. The throttles were opened to take-off power and XS783 began to roll. Initially the acceleration was as it should have been but then lessened perceptibly, resulting in a much longer run than usual to become airborne. Additionally, once unstick speed had been achieved, the climb out was sluggish. In the Air Traffic Control (ATC) tower the duty controller noticed this and radioed the pilot to check that everything was okay on board the aircraft. It wasn't, of course.

After striving skywards to a height of little more than 200 feet and a speed of 100 knots the Basset stopped climbing and accelerating. Thus the pilot's reply to his questioner was firmly in the negative and prompted the controller to press the crash alarm button, which was just as well because the pilot was at that moment struggling to cope with an emergency, as his aircraft was losing power by the second. He and his navigator colleague attempted to find the fault causing this loss of power but their efforts were in vain. With both engines spluttering, the Basset continued at a dangerously low altitude, flying over the village of Rhosneigr towards the open countryside beyond.

The reason for the machine's tardiness in becoming airborne was obvious; there was sufficient uncontaminated AVGAS lying in the fuel pipes to taxi and start the take-off run normally but moments afterwards, the engines, having consumed all the 'good' AVGAS, were drawing contaminated fuel from the aircraft's tanks, resulting in drastically reduced performance. How then could the pilot resolve a situation that was rapidly becoming critical? He was facing the dilemma of any pilot unlucky enough to experience engine failure or loss of power shortly after take-off; whether to turn back to the runway or not. Whichever choice is made, there are great risks, as we shall see.

Imagine yourself at the controls of an aircraft in this precarious condition; you have very little height, the engines have stopped delivering anything like full power and a forced landing seems inevitable. Behind you is the runway from which you have just departed, smooth and even-surfaced, quite obviously the best place by far to make an emergency landing while ahead the ground will almost certainly be more broken consisting of hedges, ditches, fields, roads, trees, buildings and suchlike. In other words, a multitude of obstacles to collide with.

Therefore, if the prospect of a safe landing is to the rear of you and danger lies in front, small wonder that turning back towards the runway appears the most attractive option. However, to speak of options is wholly misleading. The truth is that hardly any choice exists at all. For a pilot caught in this unenviable position, the golden rule is *never turn back*. Because to do so is, more often than not, to worsen an already bad situation and run the most fearful risk of inflating an emergency into a calamity. An aircraft without engine power will not have sufficient control available to complete a turn and so there is every likelyhood the machine will stall and spin into the ground. Strange though it seems, one's chances of survival are improved somewhat by continuing with a landing straight ahead and then avoiding any hazards as best as one can.

Yet so overwhelmingly powerful is the instinctive desire to reach safety almost at any cost when one's life is in danger that many pilots have ignored the advice not to attempt a turn and have done just that, only to lose their lives or be seriously injured in doing so. Some of the luckier ones have got away with it, judging they have sufficient height and speed to manouevre, though the Basset's pilot was not in this category. For him the risk was unacceptable.

While returning to Valley was therefore out of the question, another avenue became available to the hard-pressed pilot when he decided upon a diversion to RAF Mona, six miles away, but unfortunately he never reached his goal. Four miles from Valley, with the rapidly faltering Basset losing altitude and trailing black smoke, a forced landing, which had been more than probable from the start now became an immediate and inescapable reality. The landing occurred in a field near the village of Tŷ Croes. After narrowly missing a haybarn, the aircraft touched down and slid along the ground for some distance before colliding against an embankment of earth and stone. The impact destroyed the front portion of the Basset, trapping and injuring the pilot and navigator, although the Group Captain, who was also injured, managed to extricate himself from the wreckage. He then kept up the spirits of the trapped aircrew by telling them that the rescue helicopter would arrive soon.

But first on the scene was a local builder who had been driving his van along a nearby lane. He found it impossible to free the two trapped men, both of whom were conscious. Luckily, there was no post-crash fire. The would-be rescuer already had an inkling that something had happened because he noticed Valley's SAR helicopters hovering and circling near the village of Gwalchmai when he drove through only a few minutes previously. The helicopters' presence in the area was explained by the fact that Mona was close by and as this was the airfield to which the Basset was diverting, it was natural enough for the SAR crews to head towards Mona. There had been no radio contact with the stricken aircraft since the initial ATC exchanges and so the rescuers could not have known beforehand that the crash victims were in a field five miles away from the area now being searched.

It did not take long for this understandable mistake to be rectified and the helicopters were soon at the accident site, to be quickly followed by police, ambulance and fire service vehicles. It took forty-five minutes of effort to free the trapped men, who were then airlifted to hospital. Sadly, the navigator died from his injuries on the following day. He was a keen and experienced gliding enthusiast and had already survived a bad gliding accident some years previously, so it was ironic that he lost his life as a consequence of what was, in effect, a glide landing.

As for the Station Commander, his life was in greater danger than any of his rescuers had thought. Upon arrival at the hospital it was found that he had serious internal haemorrhaging and had received medical attention in the very nick of time, otherwise he would most probably have become the second victim of the crash. Although he made a full recovery, the accident affected him deeply and he never flew again.

At this point in the narrative something of a mystery has to be introduced. When the builder came upon the scene of the crash he saw not three men but four – the pilot, navigator, Station Commander, and another man. But if the Basset had only three on board, as we are led to believe from RAF sources and press accounts, who was the fourth person? And if he was not on board the aircraft, where had he come from? When the builder was asked to provide a written statement to the RAF authorities and the police, it quickly became plain to him that the authorities, for some reason, wished to play down the fact that a fourth person was at the crash site. The explanation given of the man's presence was that he was a rescuer dropped at the site by helicopter – an explanation which the recipient felt was designed to deliberately mislead him. It made no sense at all, even to a layman such as the builder, that an SAR helicopter had arrived at the scene of a serious accident and then departed, leaving a solitary crew member to cope on his own with trapped and badly injured victims.

Moreover, had he, the first witness of the crash scene, not driven through Gwalchmai village a short time previously and noticed two helicopters there? What were they doing, he reasoned, if not looking for the downed Basset? Clearly, if the SAR crews already knew, as the RAF implied they did, that the accident was at Tŷ Croes, not a moment would have been wasted searching the Gwalchmai area. The 'dropped rescuer' story did not stand up to examination, although officials strongly impressed upon a thoroughly sceptical witness that this was the truth. It was only with much reluctance that he, feeling intimidated by the authorities, accepted what he had been told. The intriguing question is why there should be this attempt to gloss over the fact that a fourth person was at the crash site. Could the explanation be that he was an unauthorised passenger, and whose presence would be embarrassing to reveal? If this was indeed the position then it was by no means the first, or the last time, that military aircraft have carried unauthorised passengers.

In 1996, in an attempt to throw some light on the mystery, the doctor responsible for treating the crash victims on their admission to the C & A Hospital at Bangor, was traced and asked if he could recall how many casualties there were. Without any prompting or a moments hesitation he replied that he saw *three* men. He clearly remembered the accident, he said, and could bring to mind many details. It seems, therefore, that the shadowy fourth man was either extremely lucky not to be injured (when all the others suffered serious injury) or else he was given medical treatment by some other, more roundabout way. Or perhaps he did not exist at all, and the official version of the story is correct. Yet the witness in this case, gaining no advantage, it must be remembered, from distorting or falsifying the truth, is so certain of what he saw with his own eyes that it is difficult to dismiss his testimony. He remains adamant that there was a fourth man at the crash scene. If he is right, as seems to be, the circumstances of the man's presence at the site remain a mystery but if the witness is wrong, then, of course, there is no mystery.

As regards the young man (twenty-six years old) who was responsible in the first place for the events leading to the crash, given the serious and ultimately fatal consequences that flowed from his actions, there was no alternative but to court martial him. He was charged with negligence in carrying out his duties. At the trial, his defending counsel, using a somewhat unfortunate choice of words in his closing speech, said that his client could be 'compared to a little robot who walked out to do what he had been asked to do.' For his part, the airman admitted that he had unthinkingly accepted the refuelling situation as it was on the day of the accident – another airman had directed the bowser to the aircraft and he, the defendant, thought his colleague had been acting correctly. Some vigilance on the part of the defendant, however, would have revealed this was not so. The airman was found guilty and ordered to be dismissed from the Service, his RAF career, sadly, at an inglorious end. Never again would he be allowed to refuel or do anything else, for that matter, to an aircraft of the Royal Air Force.

15

Wirestrike

Luckily, serious accidents to helicopters flying in Anglesey's airspace have been rare and fatal ones rarer still. In fact, by the end of the twentieth century there was only one in the latter category. Considering the frequency with which 'whirlybirds', especially the military examples operating to and from RAF Valley, are seen in the island's skies, this is quite a remarkable safety record.

Much has depended, certainly as far as the Royal Air Force is concerned, on the extremely high standard of maintenance and servicing the helicopters receive, and demand – a situation arising out of the mechanical complications inherent in all rotary-winged aircraft. These inescapable complications are centred primarily on two vital assemblies: rotors and transmission gearboxes. Not without some justification has the helicopter been described as a flying gearbox and helicopter gearboxes in general referred to as manifestations of the mechanical engineer's art in its highest form!

It was in 1955, when 'C' Flight of 22 Squadron, a Search and Rescue (SAR) unit operating Westland Whirlwinds came to Valley that helicopters became a regular feature of the aviation scene in Anglesey. Since then they and their successors (the Wessex in 1976 and Sea King in 1997) established themselves as an almost integral part of the island's life and there is hardly an Anglesey resident who has not seen these helicopters, in their distinctive yellow livery, at one time or another.

As mentioned already, the safety record of helicopters operating in Anglesey has been second to none and it was not until 25 November 1963 that the first accident occurred. This was when Westland Whirlwind XD164 from the RAF's Central Flying School (CFS) got into trouble near Holyhead. The helicopter was practising homing on to a radio beacon when the engine lost power and the machine was autorotated (the equivalent of a glide in a fixed-wing aircraft) into the sea 200 yards from shore at a point one mile north of the causeway linking Anglesey with Holy Island (and Holyhead). Within five minutes one of Valley's SAR Whirlwinds was on the scene and rescued the four-man crew, who were unharmed.

Six year later, almost to the day of the Holyhead accident, another accident involving a CFS Whirlwind, XP343, took place, on Wednesday 26 November 1969. This machine took off from Valley on a training flight but crashed shortly after becoming airborne when the rotor struck a roof, the tail then hit the ground and broke off. Fortunately, harm to the crew was minimal – one man suffered a minor injury to his shoulder. In the 1970s there were only two accidents to military helicopters and both resulted in ditchings. The first was on Wednesday, 13 December 1972 when one of 22 Squadron's Whirlwinds, XP349, ditched in Holyhead harbour following engine failure and the second incident was on Wednesday, 20 September 1978 when a Royal Navy Wessex, XP143, of 737 Squadron ditched fifteen miles off Holyhead whilst en route from Prestwick to Valley. The four men in the Wessex were rescued by 22 Squadron and the helicopter subsequently salvaged.

There was only one accident in the 1980s, when Westland/Aerospatiale Gazelle ZB627 of No.2 FTS, RAF Shawbury experienced a birdstrike on Wednesday, 2 September 1987. After the collision, believed to be with a seagull, the Gazelle's perspex canopy was shattered, causing cuts and bruises to the pilot. He made a safe landing on Aberffraw Common. His two colleagues were unhurt but it is unlikely the same could be said for the unlucky seagull.

In the 1990s the situation was further improved over the preceding decade, with nothing more than one near-accident, though if it had taken place it would probably have been very serious. The date was Friday, 6 February 1998. On that day a

Westland/Aerospatiale Puma helicopter, XW198, (which, incidentally, was the first British production Puma) of 230 Squadron, RAF Aldergrove, was at Valley, prior to making a return flight to Northern Ireland. At the time of the incident, the Puma was being refuelled in readiness for the coming flight but the refuel was of the 'rotors running' type. That is, while fuel was being pumped into the helicopter's tanks the machine's twin engines were delivering power to the rotor, which was revolving. This was a potentially hazardous situation. Being close to a helicopter's spinning rotors is always dangerous and to undertake the task of refuelling a helicopter under these conditions doubles the danger. Not only is there a risk of being struck by the rotor blades but there is also a strong risk of fire.

To increase the safety of a 'rotors running' refuel a fire tender is positioned close to the helicopter, ready to spring into instant action in the event of a fire. This was the case at Valley on 6 February. A fire tender was present, located in front of the Puma and pointing directly towards it. Of the Puma's three crew, the captain was in the operations building, planning the flight to Aldergrove, the Air Loadmaster was alongside the helicopter supervising the refuelling and the second pilot was at the aircraft's controls. When the refuelling operation was completed the pilot gave the clearance signal for the bowser and fire tender to move away but as the driver of the fire tender engaged gear he heard a loud bang from the rear of his vehicle and it then lurched forward violently towards the Puma. Immediately, the pilot applied full power to lift the helicopter into a hover, clear of the danger. There was no time for any take-off checks to be made and so the autopilot was not engaged, forcing the pilot to control what was a highly unstable machine. His speedy reaction had undoubtedly prevented a serious accident from taking place. If the fire tender had collided with the Puma then almost certainly the latter would have been destroyed. Both its pilot and the fire tender's driver might have been killed or seriously injured. Additionally, in a worst case scenario, it was possible for the bowser, standing nearby, to be hit by pieces of the disintegrating rotor blades thus causing an explosion which would have engulfed the whole area in burning fuel. Fortunately none of this happened, thanks to the professionalism and flying skill of the Puma's quick-thinking pilot.

Let us now turn to the one accident in Anglesey which resulted in fatalities. The machine involved was a civilian helicopter and its downfall came about through a wirestrike – a collision with power cables. Helicopters, because they usually fly low, are particularly prone to wirestrikes and as there are poles and pylons more or less everywhere, supporting electricity lines, helicopter pilots have to be especially vigilant in this respect. If they are not, then disaster can strike, as it did on Thursday, 25 October 1979. Shortly after 9.30 a.m. a Hughes 269C light helicopter, registered G-BBIU, landed on the helipad at the Rhosgoch oil storage complex owned by the giant multinational company, Shell. Crude oil which had been pumped ashore from supertankers moored at a marine terminal at the nearby port of Amlwch was stored in huge tanks at Rhosgoch before being pumped through an underground pipeline which ran along the North Wales coast to the company's refinery at Stanlow, in Cheshire. This pipeline, ninety-eight miles long, had to be inspected every fortnight and it was the duty of G-BBIU's two-man crew to carry out this task on that particular Thursday. Piloting the Hughes 269C was a young man, only 22-years old though with 501 hours entered in his flying log, 268 of those hours being on helicopters. He had landed at Rhosgoch, to which he had flown on a number of previous occasions, in order to pick up a Shell employee who would carry out the actual inspection. The employee was a 42-year old local man from the nearby village of Penygroes, who, besides his work for Shell, was also making a name for himself as a singer and entertainer, having appeared many times on Welsh television.

The start of the pipeline, where that morning's inspection

would begin, was 400 metres from the helipad but inbetween there ran a line of high-voltage power cables. These cables, to quote from the accident report ' . . . were not easy to see against the background of a small ridge.' In fact, they were well nigh impossible to see. Viewed from the helipad they were below the skyline and so well camouflaged by fields and hedges as to become practically invisible. To make matters worse, because of local topography, there was very little height difference (only a few metres) between the helipad and the cables at their lowest point. They were almost level with the helipad and in a position that a pilot would not have expected power lines to be. On the other hand, the supporting pylons were plainly visible.

After the passenger had boarded the helicopter, it lifted off normally and hover-taxied slowly for fifty metres before accelerating away, but within a few seconds the *thwack-thwack* of its rotor blades ended suddenly and disastrously when the machine collided with the cables. There is little doubt that the pilot failed to see the obstruction which lay in his path. After the wirestrike G-BBIU broke up and fell to the ground, throwing both men clear of the wreckage. The pipeline inspector was dead, while his colleague was very badly injured.

Firefighters from the oil storage site were quickly on the scene but there was no post-crash fire for them to tackle. Although fuel had leaked from the wrecked helicopter, this fuel had not ignited. Two Wessex helicopters from RAF Valley also arrived soon after the accident. On board one was Valley's Senior Medical Officer, who spent fifteen minutes attempting, without success, to resuscitate the injured pilot, who, sadly, later died in hospital.

On the following day accident investigators from the Department of Transport's Air Accidents Investigation Branch (AAIB) arrived to examine the wreckage and discovered that the victims had been thrown from their seats because the quick-release fastenings of their harnesses became undone during the crash. The harnesses were fitted in 1978 in accordance with a

Civil Aviation Authority (CAA) requirement for upper torso restraint but following the loss of G-BBIU there was close scrutiny of the design and the subsequent discovery of its shortcomings. As a result, the CAA required all operators of the Hughes 269 and 369 series of helicopters to replace the faulty buckles or complete harness with those of a different design. However, as far as the two men involved in the Rhosgoch accident were concerned, stronger harness fastenings would not have made any difference. The crash was not survivable.

The obvious question to arise out of this tragedy is why the pilot failed to notice the power cables? Most of the answer lies in the fact that these cables were so hard to see against a background of foliage and greenery. Yet the pilot was familiar with the area after his previous visits to Rhosgoch and he had flown safely on all previous occasions. Additionally, we have to ask ourselves why he appeared not to have spotted the strong visual indication of danger provided by the pylons. While the cables themselves were well hidden, the structures supporting them were not and so their presence, one would expect, would have led the pilot to assume that strung out between each pylon were lengths of wire which had to be avoided at all costs. Plainly, this did not happen and thus was missed a visual clue which might well have saved the helicopter from the calamitous wirestrike which it suffered.

16

Gnat Crashes

In November 1962 No.4 Flying Training School, based at Valley, which by then was one of the RAF's most important training airfields, took delivery of a new type of aircraft to replace the ageing de Havilland Vampires which had served the School so well for over a decade. The replacement was the Hawker Siddeley Gnat, a diminutive swept-wing jet aircraft developed originally in the early 1950s as a fighter by W.E.W. Petter (or 'Teddy' as he was known), chief designer at Folland Ltd. Teddy Petter was regarded as a designer of genius but at the same time he possessed an unworldy quality and had a reputation for being difficult to deal with.

His hopes of seeing the Gnat enter service as a fighter were dashed when the RAF chose not to select the machine (it had been overtaken by the Hawker Hunter) though despite this setback, further design studies showed the aircraft had potential as a two-seater advanced trainer. This was to be the Gnat's future. An extra seat in tandem was added, the fuselage lengthened, wing area increased, as was the tailplane and fin, the air intakes were redesigned and extra fuel capacity added. This additional capacity was just as well because the jet's Bristol Siddeley Orpheus engine proved to be exceptionally thirsty. The prototype Gnat trainer (XM691) first flew in August 1959. Shortly after this first flight Folland was taken over by the Hawker Siddeley Group – a move strongly opposed by Petter, who, disillusioned and bitter, then abandoned the aircraft industry for ever and retired, with his family, to Switzerland. There he led, in his own words, 'a simple life of prayer and meditation', dressed in a monk-like habit. He died in 1968. Such was the man responsible for the genesis of the Gnat, an aircraft which featured so prominently in the skies of Anglesey during the 1960s and 1970s.

Deliveries of the new trainer to Valley were completed by August 1963, by which time the Anglesey airfield had a fleet of eighty-nine aircraft. But once in service, the Gnat turned out to be rather disappointing and there were many difficulties. Poor serviceability, for example, was a major problem, initially at least, with frequent failures of the electrical system and powered controls. The aircraft became the despair of many an Engineering Officer and few would have disagreed with the opinion of one Chief Technician who said that, ' . . . engineering-wise [the Gnat] was a nightmare.' Additionally, there were other difficulties of a more operational kind: a high accident rate, limited visibility from the rear cockpit, restricted endurance and excessive fuel consumption. This latter point was addressed on the very first page of Training Command's *Gnat Student Study Guide*; ' . . . When flying at range speed at sea level the Gnat uses fuel at *twice* [author's italics] the rate of the Jet Provost . . . Constant orientation and fuel consciousness are therefore vital.' Then the *Guide* goes on to explain that, 'The aircraft has delightful flying characteristics', though in the same breath adding a warning that, 'The work load when flying a Gnat is high . . . and things happen fast.' In other words, the Gnat could be something of a handful and not only for students but instructors also. As one commented, it was 'a twitchy machine that needed a lot of flying'. Another, a highly experienced pilot, when asked by the present writer if he had ever had to deal with an emergency in the Gnat replied, '*Every* Gnat pilot had an emergency!'

One of the major weaknesses of the aircraft was its hydraulically operated control system, which was complex and not always reliable, the tailplane in particular proving to be troublesome. It was prone to sudden failure and became something of an Achilles' Heel for the Gnat. The technical intracies of the control system are far beyond the scope of the present volume but suffice it to say that the aircraft had a flying tail, that is, tailplane and the elevators were normally locked together and moved under hydraulic power as one unit in response to stick movements. Activating this flying tail was a mechanism known as the 'K' cam and 'Q' gear (so-called because engineers had used all the preceding letters of the alphabet naming unsuccessful designs before a workable solution had been found).

The 'K' cam and 'Q' gear mechanism dominated the life of every pilot who encountered the Gnat and an actual example of the infamous mechanism is permanently displayed at Valley, where the exhibit has been mounted on a piece of varnished wood and hung on the wall of the History Room in the Station's headquarters building. Above the display are the words;

Confusing at first
When initially told
Quite simple really
Gnaturally controlled

Beneath are the following lines;

Dedicated to all students who
sorted out their cam 'K'from
their 'Q' gear.

Another problem in the re-designed Gnat was that the Centre of Gravity altered dramatically when the undercarriage was operated, and to counter this problem an automatic datum shift had to be incorporated into the design. Upon lowering of the undercarriage, the tailplane angle of incidence was changed three and a half degrees in the 'nose-up' sense, with the reverse occurring when the undercarriage was raised. These changes were brought about by means of a chain ('little more than a bicycle chain', said one Valley pilot) connected to the starboard wheel, but this mechanical linkage still required hydraulic pressure at the tailplane for the datum shift to work, and this, in fact, was the nub of the problem. Hydraulic failure could create such control difficulties for a pilot, especially at critical periods, when landing, for example, that the only alternative was to abandon the aircraft.

The intractable tailplane difficulties of the Gnat brought about the loss of many aircraft, though, of course, not all the twenty-nine losses during the type's period of service at Valley were due to this particular problem but it did result in a number of changes to the training syllabus. Areas of operation accessible to students in the 1960s had, by the early 1970s, become open only to instructors, the most notable example being forced landings in manual. The judgement required to carry out this exercise, bearing in mind the Gnat's complexities, had been too much for some students, resulting in heavy landings and by 1972 only QFIs could carry out practise manual forced landings.

To deal chronologically and briefly with some of the Gnat accidents in Anglesey, the first was on Tuesday, 10 December 1963, when XP542 made a landing with its nose-wheel up. At the controls was the Wing Commander in charge of flying operations at Valley. He brought the aircraft to a halt almost undamaged. Many years later, in the 1970s he would return to Valley as the Station Commander but sadly he was to die when still relatively young through leukaemia, brought on, it seems likely, after his participation in the British nuclear weapons testing programmes at Christmas Island in the South Pacific during the 1950s.

The next Gnat loss was that of XR976 on Monday, 12 October 1964. The aircraft, flown by two QFIs, Flight Lieutenant Mike Vickers and a Royal Navy officer, Lt. Richard Sheridan, made a heavy landing on runway 32, became airborne once again but quickly became uncontrollable. At a height of 300 feet the occupants ejected and landed safely on the airfield, leaving the Gnat to its fate. It flew in a circle to the left, coming close to Rhosneigr before crashing amongst low sand dunes some 200 yards from the clubhouse of the Rhosneigr Golf Club, the actual point of impact being close to a footbridge spanning a small river, the Afon Crigyll, which meanders through this sandy area to reach the nearby sea. The *North Wales Chronicle* (16 October 1964) commented, 'People living in a row of houses at Rhosneigr had a lucky escape on Monday afternoon when a Folland Gnat jet aircraft narrowly missed the houses and crashed into sand dunes less than half a mile away.'

On Thursday, 14 January 1965, the accident was more or less repeated when XR568 undershot and crashed in the very same dunes, again only a few hundred yards from Rhosneigr Golf Club and again involving one of the pilots who had ejected from XR976 three months previously – Flight Lieutenant Vickers. He was accompanied on this second occasion by a fellow-instructor, Flight Lieutenant Paul Wilson, undergoing refresher training after a period away from flying. At 2.15 p.m. the pair took off from runway 26 and had only reached a height of 700 feet when the Gnat's engine failed. The two pilots decided to turn downwind for runway 32 but undershot, probably because of the strong wind that was blowing and adversely affecting their now-unpowered aircraft. Landing close to the Crigyll river, the Gnat then bounced over this gentle, slow-moving stretch of water and came to a stop only fifty yards from the airfield's boundary fence. Here there were concrete posts, one of which caught the port slipper tank of the Gnat and ripped it off. The tank erupted into flames though the rest of the aircraft did not catch fire, luckily for Paul Wilson sitting in the front cockpit. He was trapped in the wreckage by his legs and if a fire had occurred he would have been burnt to death. Rescue crews from Valley were at the scene of the accident within minutes but it took nearly an hour for them to free the trapped pilot. When he was finally released from the wreckage he was found to have a broken leg. His companion, Mike Vickers, was unhurt.

Some of Rhosneigr's residents were greatly disturbed by these crashes and others that were to follow. Eventually a committee of residents was formed to fight what they regarded as the serious threat posed to the safety of Rhosneigr by flying operations at Valley. During the mid and late 1960s the committee was to become a thorn in the flesh of the Station Commander.

On Tuesday, 9 March 1965, XR542 crashed on approach, whilst XR985 was badly damaged in a crash on Monday, 5 April. More serious was a mid-air collision only a few weeks later when, on Thursday, 22 April, XS108 and XR950, as part of a three-ship formation, collided over Carmel, near Caernarfon. The latter aircraft crashed near Carmel, killing the QFI pilot, while the former machine, flown by a student, came back in a damaged condition to Valley. The student was badly advised to attempt a landing (he should have been ordered to eject) and a few minutes later he made a fast – much too fast – approach to runway 32 (when he had been told to use runway 14). There was little chance of maintaining control over the damaged aircraft at the speed with which it touched down and as a result it crashed halfway along the runway, killing the pilot, (see the author's *Aircraft Crashes, Flying Accidents in Gwynedd 1910-1990* for a full account of this tragic accident).

Then, almost three months to the day of the Carmel mid-air collision and the death of two pilots, a third was killed on Monday 19 July when the Gnat (XR543) he was piloting crashed into Maelog Lake, on the edge of Rhosneigr. The aircraft was on approach to land at Valley and was being flown solo by a 20-year old student. He had stalled the Gnat during the final approach. In reporting the accident, the *North Wales Chronicle* (23 July 1965), besides reminding readers of the closeness of houses to the crash site – 'the lake is bounded . . . by a large caravan site and a number of private houses' – also had an interesting footnote;

'The manufacturers . . . have said the Gnat is no more accident prone than the Vampire, which was considered a successful jet trainer. A spokesman for the firm said; "There is nothing wrong with the aircraft, [the accident rate] is due to the inexperience of the men who fly [the Gnats]." '

Whilst in the particular case of XR543 there may have been some truth in this statement, generally the distinction between pilot errors and faulty machines was not quite so sharply defined. Few companies like to admit that their product is defective in any way and it was obvious that Hawker Siddeley was not going to explain the complexities of the 'K' cam and 'Q' gear to the *North Wales Chronicle*. Yet another Gnat accident took place on Monday, 6 September 1965, when XR979, moments after becoming airborne, crashed back on to the runway. The instant the aircraft came to a halt its sole occupant jumped out and ran, leaving his mount to burst into flames. 'Pilot Leaps to Safety' said the *North Wales Chronicle* (10 September 1965), 'Did that fellow run!', said one observer to the author, 'an Olympic medallist wouldn't have beaten him'.

During the following year, there was a fatal accident when, on Wednesday, 13 April XP507 crashed on Cymyran beach after experiencing a failure of the tailplane whilst on approach to land on runway 02. Sadly, both occupants of the aircraft, an instructor and his student, were killed.

The next incident involving a Gnat at Valley (though there had been other crashes in the North Wales region, but which are outside the scope of the present volume) was on Wednesday, 23 August 1967, when XP512 came to grief, as in the case of XP507, because of tailplane failure. At this point the writer has to declare a stronger than usual interest in this accident because, as mentioned in the Introduction, it was an accident he personally witnessed. It is easier, therefore, to continue the narrative by disregarding literary convention and reverting to the use of the first person singular in the following account of the incident, as seen through the author's eyes.

'During the afternoon of that Wednesday I was in one of the upper storey offices of the Gaydon Hangar, the Engineering Wing's centre of operations at Valley. It was a fine, warm afternoon, with the airfield as busy as ever: Gnats taking off, landing, taxying, pilots walking to and from their aircraft on the

Flight Line, Flight Handlers going about their various duties, marshalling, helping crews into and out of cockpits, checking this and checking that, refuelling bowsers trundling along to replenish empty fuel tanks in the ever-thirsty jets, while many assorted vehicles, RAF jeeps, towing tractors etc. could be seen moving around the airfield.

'Suddenly this activity was interrupted by two bangs, plainly audible to me in the triple-glazed office I was in (designed to keep the noise from aircraft on the nearby Flight Line down to a reasonably tolerable level). Then, almost in the same instant the crash alarm sounded – its raucous, insistent stridency impossible to ignore. In this situation there was only one course of action I could take; rush outside to see what was happening. This I did, along with everybody else in the building. When the crash alarm went, nobody wanted to miss out on seeing the action.

'I ran the few yards along the corridor to where the external fire escape stairs were located. Standing at the top of these stairs I had a good view of the airfield and the first thing I saw was a figure dangling from an orange-coloured parachute floating down from a height of a few hundred feet above the ground. Behind, and slightly above him there was a second parachutist. Clearly, this was the explanation for the bangs I heard – two pilots had ejected from a Gnat – but where was the aircraft?

'I looked to my right and there it was, still airborne and wallowing along, riding the air currents as a free spirit for the first – and last – time. To my consternation I noticed that the Gnat was heading directly towards Rhosneigr and if, as seemed likely, the aircraft was going to crash on the village, what, I wondered, would be the result? The very thought appalled me. Of one thing I was certain. Regardless of whether there was going to be any loss of life or not, if that aircraft did crash on Rhosneigr then an almighty row was sure to erupt. Knowing what a sensitive issue the nuisance created by flying operations at Valley was to some of the village's residents, I could foresee angry deputations to the Station Commander, banner headlines in the press, the involvement of Anglesey's MP and even questions asked in Parliament. A veritable hornet's nest of protest would be unleashed. These were the thoughts racing through my mind as I watched the Gnat pitching and yawing crazily towards Rhosneigr. Then the aircraft seemed to lose altitude and I lost sight of it as it disappeared from view behind sand dunes.

'For me that was the end of the action – there was little else to be seen and so I returned to the office. Afterwards, I learnt that the Gnat had come down on Rhosneigr beach, landing in three feet of water and in doing so seemed to have suffered surprisingly little damage, outwardly at least.

'As for the two pilots, the trainee was unhurt, while his instructor, a New Zealander, had been unlucky enough to break both his legs. He was in the Station Sick Quarters within one minute, following instant rescue by a 22 Squadron helicopter which just happened to be airborne over the airfield at the time. The Gnat was on an instructional sortie when the tailplane went into a 'runaway' condition (the intricacies and weaknesses of the Gnat tailplane have already been referred to) and had gone the maximum possible of twelve degrees 'up', (a tailplane could only runaway in the 'up' position). The result was a strong, not to say overwhelming tendency for the aircraft to climb. To counter this tendency the occupants needed their combined strength to push the stick hard forward and at the same time full power was applied. In this condition the Gnat had an airspeed of 140 knots or so. It was virtually impossible to land the disabled jet with any degree of safety, of course, leaving the instructor and his student no alternative but to eject. They pointed the Gnat out to sea and then fired their seats. But, as I had witnessed, the abandoned aircraft flew towards Rhosneigr. With full power on and in a marked 'nose-up' attitude the Gnat remained airborne. Then it stalled, a wing dropped, and the aircraft continued in the air. This action was repeated three times before the machine finally came down in shallow water on Rhosneigr beach.

Luckily, none of the holidaymakers on the beach were injured though some had had a narrow escape. One teenage girl was only ten feet from the aircraft when it hit the water. For two people on that beach watching the Gnat was a particular horror. They were a married couple from Stockport, who lived very close to the scene of the crash of an airliner (a Canadair C-4 Argonaut, G-ALHG belonging to British Midland Airways) on the middle of the town only two months previously, on 4 June. Seventy two people lost their lives in that disaster and the Stockport couple, whilst observing the Gnat's final moments thought they were going to be caught in the middle of another tragedy. Thankfully, they were wrong.

'On the following day the Gnat was recovered and dumped in a corner of the Engineering Wing hangar. I was eager to have a close look but there were too many airmen on the hangar floor for my liking and I was afraid my inquisitiveness would result in a sharp reminder from some 'Chiefy' (Chief Technician) or NCO to mind my own business. However, on the next day, a Friday, few people were about by late afternoon and so I decided this was my opportunity to do some snooping. I walked quickly towards the jet and my first impression of the machine was how undamaged it appeared to be. Besides a broken off nose cone there were no other visible signs of damage which I could detect. I felt sure XP512 would soon be in the air once more. Mine was an inexpert eye, of course, and my assessment was entirely wrong; the Gnat was destined never to fly again. It was struck off charge on 1 September.

'I had not been standing in the hangar for very long when I noticed an officer striding purposefully towards me. I recognised him as Squadron Leader C........, the second-in-command of the Flying Wing at Valley. Fully expecting to be ordered away from the aircraft, I waited for the Squadron Leader to speak. To my surprise he completely ignored me and proceeded to look over the Gnat. Therefore, I remained where I was, though feeling decidedly uncomfortable, hoping perhaps that he might wish to converse and share a few thoughts but he did not utter a single word, whilst I, for my part, was unable to summon up enough courage to speak to him.

'I was fascinated, however, by the expression on his face as he inspected the aircraft. His look had a most curious ambivalance. Was it a smile or a grimace? I could not make up my mind. I wondered what the man was thinking; relief that he was not the pilot on this occasion, coupled with an awareness that he could well be the next victim, given the Gnat's shortcomings, or perhaps it was just the mixed feelings of a professional aviator when confronted with a crashed aircraft – an unpleasant reminder of what can happen if things go wrong in the air.'

Later that year, on Thursday, 14 December, XP509 belly landed at Valley and was eventually struck off charge. There were no further serious accidents or fatalities in Anglesey during the 1960s but the 1970s started badly when, on the morning of Saturday, 3 January 1970, XR997 suffered hydraulic failure on taking off and crashed soon after on buildings belonging to Tŷ Mawr Farm, Llanfaelog. An instructor and his student lost their lives but the farmer's two teenage sons had a lucky escape. 'We were in the farmyard', one said, 'carrying buckets from the dairy to the piggery and we had just left the dairy when there was a screaming sound. There was a terrific crash just behind us. The aircraft crashed into the field and then bounced into the buildings, setting fire to hay and demolishing the dairy.' Three calves and seven pigs were killed. More fortunate was the farmer's dog, a six-months old Labrador named Mick. Although very close to the Gnat when it crashed he received nothing worse than a soaking in kerosene, spilled from the doomed aircraft's tanks. Mick reeked of jet fuel for days afterwards but at least he was alive.

Three years later, XP508 crashed on Thursday, 6 September

when it suffered loss of power on take-off. It was being flown by Valley's test pilot, newly arrived from RAF Wattisham, where he had been flying Lightnings. The flight in XP508 was, in fact, his first Gnat air test. At the time of his appointment to his new job, however, his domestic situation was in turmoil, his wife having just left him. From a flight safety viewpoint the resultant stress and emotional upheaval of a marital break-up was not good. Such factors can and have been known to have an adverse effect upon a pilot's performance.

On the day of the accident, before climbing into the Gnat's cockpit, the 32-year old pilot followed the time-honoured (and absolutely essential) procedure of the 'walk round', the pre-flight visual inspection of the aircraft's external surfaces, flying controls, air intakes and wheels etc. It is a vital check to ensure that there are no loose panels, hydraulic leaks or suchlike to create an emergency once airborne. In the case of XP508 the pilot took an unusually long time to complete his walk round – a fact noticed by the groundcrew. Having satisfied himself that nothing was amiss he eased himself into the cramped front cockpit of the jet. But despite his lengthy inspection he had missed something. Lying inside one of the air intakes was a small jubilee clip.

After engine start the pilot called for taxi clearance, was given it, taxied out to runway 20, called for take-off clearance, was given it, and then, at 12.40 p.m., began his take-off roll. Within a few moments there was a loud bang and the engine began to run down. It had ingested the jubilee clip. There was time to abort the take-off but the pilot chose to continue and managed to coax the aircraft to a height of 300 feet above Cymyran Bay before starting to turn back towards the airfield. This manoeuvre resulted in a loss of airspeed, for which there was insufficient engine power to compensate and the Gnat stalled. At this point the pilot ejected, though sadly he did not survive. He came down in the waters of Cymyran Bay (as did the aircraft) where he drowned before the SAR helicopter could get to him. His time as Valley's test pilot had been tragically short-lived.

A further loss was that of XR571, which was damaged beyond repair whilst landing on Tuesday, 28 October 1975. The accident was caused by PIO – Pilot Induced Oscillation. There were, of course, other Gnat losses during the 1970s but they were outside the geographical boundaries of Anglesey and so are omitted from the present volume. Amongst the worst was the mid-air collision between XR983 and XP536 on Friday, 30 April 1976 near the village of Brithdir, in Merionethshire. Four pilots were killed, one of whom, Flight Lieutenant Graham Ivell, was a schoolfriend of the author during the 1950s.

Two weeks after the September 1973 accident to XP508, Flight Lieutenant Douglas Mee, a pilot based at RAF Oakington, was telephoned by Valley's Station Commander and asked if he would like the job of unit test pilot. Mee was no stranger to Valley. He had spent a tour of duty there during the Vampire era of the 1950s and had been a member of the aerobatic team. A return to the Anglesey airfield appealed to him and he decided to accept the Station Commander's offer.

For the next five years he flew 4 FTS' Gnats without incident, that is until Tuesday, 7 February 1978, when the aircraft he was piloting failed him. On that day he was practising flapless approaches and landings in Gnat XR541, using the runway at RAF Mona. Accompanying Mee was a friend and colleague, a QFI at Valley who had come along 'just for the ride' – a common practice amongst the instructors if there was a spare seat available on a sortie because such flights allowed flying hours to be maximised and therefore flying experience also.

The approach and landing immediately preceding the accident had been in accordance with Pilot's Notes; 'Carry out a wider circuit than normal, starting the final turn at a minimum speed of 170 knots.' Without flaps the touch-down of XR541 was at a faster speed than normal, 165 knots instead of the usual 135 knots, although this did not matter very much because it was

Mee's intention to perform a 'roller', that is, to let the aircraft roll for a short period before taking off once again. But when the Gnat's throttle was opened to take-off power, alarmingly, nothing happened. The engine just seemed to stagnate, leaving the pilot in a very difficult position.

His aircraft was thundering down the runway at the proverbial rate of knots (165 knots is equal to a speed of 186 mph!) yet unable to achieve flight because of insufficient engine power. The only alternative was to brake to a halt, though this goal was as difficult to attain as the first. So high was the jet's speed and so much of the runway had been consumed by the time braking commenced that it was impossible to stop the Gnat before reaching the end of the tarmac. An arrester barrier engagement was, therefore, inevitable. The aircraft, with its forward impetus hardly checked by braking, plunged headlong into the barrier, whose slats were unable to cope with the load imposed upon them by the fast moving Gnat, which then broke through the barrier, left the tyre-marked runway and speeded towards the airfield's boundary fence, with the jet's wheels making deep furrows in the ground.

As Flight Lieutenant Mee said, 'Things didn't look too good for us at that moment!' But the barrier did not fail completely; the upper support wire – an inch thick steel hawser – slid over the aircraft and caught the bottom of the tailfin at the point where it joined the fuselage. When the wire bit deep into the metal, it exerted a downward pull on the tail which pushed up the nose sufficiently for the aircraft to become momentarily airborne before it crunched back on to the ground and continued relentlessly onwards to the airfield boundary. The steel hawser did its work of retardation well, while still not completely arresting the momentum of the Gnat, which ran on until it hit the boundary hedge. This collision finally brought the aircraft to a halt.

Luckily, Mee was unhurt. His immediate concern after the jet stopped was for his colleague in the back seat. Using the intercom, he asked him if he was alright but there was no reply. Convinced that this silence indicated injury and unconsciousness Mee swiftly undid his harness, jumped out of his seat and was greeted, to his immense relief, by his friend's smiling face as he looked out over the edge of the cockpit. 'I'm not bloody well flying with *you* again!', was the friend's joking response.

Inspection of XR541 after the crash revealed the second pilot had a lucky escape from disaster. After the Gnat's brief leap into the air, the impact with which it made contact with the ground subsequently had driven the nosewheel up into its housing with such force that it caused the rear cockpit floor, which lay above the housing, to distort upwards to such an extent that it was almost touching the ejection seat's lower firing handle wire. This wire runs underneath the seat and connects the operating handle at the front to the firing mechanism at the rear. If the cockpit floor had been pushed up just a fraction further it would have exerted pressure on this wire and most probably caused the seat to fire.

As the Gnat ejection seat was intended for use only at speeds above ninety knots, accidental operation could have had unpleasant consequences for the occupant of the rear cockpit. However, he lived to fly another day, though only two months later he had another bad experience when he and his student were forced to abandon XR544, on Wednesday, 26 April. The aircraft suffered engine malfunction when only 270 feet above the ground on final approach to runway 14 at Valley. Roller bearings in the fuel pump drive shaft had failed, allowing the shaft to disconnect from the pump. The instructor survived this second accident also, though with some slight injury to his back and a much changed outlook on life. The close shave in XR541 and then only two months later having to eject from XR544 had a profound effect upon the man. Twice within two months he had come almost face to face with the Grim Reaper and twice he had evaded his clutches. The pilot attributed this to Divine Providence, no less, and became a much more spiritual person.

In fact, the accident to XR544 turned out to be the last in Anglesey as by then the Gnat's period of service was rapidly drawing to a close.

As for XR541, it was never restored to an airworthy condition. The broken machine was stripped of all its useful components and the shell deposited in a hangar corner, where it lay for the remainder of the year. In December it was transported from Anglesey to RAF St. Athan to become an instructional airframe in the Civilian Craft Apprentices' School. Interestingly enough, the very last flying accident to occur in Anglesey during the twentieth century was an almost exact repeat of that experienced by XR541. On Tuesday, 24 August 1999, Hawk XX160 was at Mona practising circuits when it suffered a birdstike at the moment the pilot was about to take off. He made a quick decision to abort the take off and the aircraft had a barrier engagement. This eventually brought the jet to a halt after having just penetrated the boundary fence on the Bodffordd side of the airfield, just as XR541 did in 1978. The Hawk's pilot was unhurt but shaken. His aircraft was not seriously damaged.

By 1979 the Gnat era was at an end. On 24 November that year the final Gnat course graduated and it was a date set to coincide with the official withdrawal of the aircraft from RAF service. Two weeks earlier Valley's Chief Instructor had led a formation of twelve Gnats on a tour of North Wales coastal towns to mark sixteen years of flying training. Since training began on the Gnat in 1963 the type had flown more than 157,000 hours at Valley and trained 1,421 students. But the question has to be asked, was it a good training aircraft? As we have seen, the Gnat was never an easy aircraft to fly and there were many difficulties, previously enumerated – difficulties such as poor serviceability, a restricted view from the cockpit and limited endurance, all of which combined to reduce the aircraft's effectiveness.

Although officially the Gnat was regarded as a successful

trainer, some privately expressed views were rather more mixed. For example, the frustrations faced by one protesting QFI were put most graphically by him; 'The instructor's position in the rear cockpit was like that of a woman trying to give birth in a dustbin.' On the other hand, there was a view amongst some QFIs that if a student could fly the Gnat then he could also fly the Lightning – the front-line fighter which many of Valley's output of pilots would go on to fly. Perhaps the fairest assessment of the Gnat is that like a partner in a stagnant marriage it was tolerated rather than loved.

17

Mid-Air Collision

During the first weekend of August 1972 a dentist's wife left the family home in Upton-by-Chester and travelled to Anglesey, where she and her husband had a caravan at the Silver Bay Caravan Park, Rhoscolyn. Accompanying the 51-year old woman were two teenage girls; the woman's daughter, aged 14 and the daughter's friend, also aged 14. The plan was that the woman would spend the first seven days of a three-week holiday without her husband, who would then join her and the two teenage girls at Rhoscolyn for the remaining fortnight, to enjoy the sea, sand and sunshine of Anglesey. However, fate decreed that it was not to be.

When the dentist said goodbye to his wife as she set off for North Wales, it was to be the last time he would see her alive. The couple's parting turned out to be permanent rather than temporary and their fond *au revoir* was, had they but known it, an *adieu* and was, in truth, a prelude to tragedy.

That tragedy happened a few days later at Silver Bay, which is located on the same stretch of coast as RAF Valley – the former being some two miles to the west of the latter. This particular caravan park is no different to any of the others dotted around the island except perhaps for the fact that its residents have access to a secluded private beach tucked into a small bay which gives its name to the park. This bay is close to Valley, being separated from the western extremity of the airfield by nothing more than a small, low-lying area of rocky coastline and a narrow creek.

It is a closeness which, arguably, gives Silver Bay its only disadvantage; the air is frequently rent by the sound of jets taking off from and landing at Valley, as they were doing on Thursday, 10 August, a day when the caravan site's holiday atmosphere was to be shattered in a horrific manner. The weather was good, with early morning sunshine soon coaxing many of the Park's 600 residents from their wheeled abodes. By lunchtime most of the site's 175 caravans were empty, their occupants either enjoying themselves at the nearby beach or out and about, exploring the nooks and crannies of Anglesey and visiting places of interest. In other words, a typical day at the height of the tourist season but at Rhoscolyn the day was soon to take on an entirely different and grimmer aspect.

During the early part of the afternoon, it was estimated that some 100 people were on the site, including the Cheshire dentist's wife and the two young girls in her charge. All three were in their caravan. Shortly before 2.00 p.m. the girls went to a toilet block which was some distance away, leaving the older female on her own. It was a few minutes later, at 2.00 p.m., that the catastrophe occurred.

There was a loud bang followed by a whooshing noise and then the caravan was subjected to an impact as if it was being pushed and prodded by the fingers of an angry but invisible giant. At the same time, the vehicle was engulfed in flames which immediately set it on fire, with its occupant – the middle-aged woman – still inside. For her, an ordinary, peaceful afternoon had, entirely without warning, and within the space of a few, brief seconds turned into a hideous, terror-filled nightmare. Sadly, the severe burns she received in the fire, together with the large amounts of poisonous carbon monoxide inhaled by her proved fatal and she died.

The woman's daughter also heard the bang and on emerging from the toilet block she saw smoke in a nearby field. She then gained higher ground to obtain a better view and saw, to her horror, that the caravan she had just vacated was in flames. It was the start of the young girl's agony because what she was looking at was, in effect, the funeral pyre of her mother. The shocked teenager could see two other caravans burning besides that of her parents and there were also other areas of fire on the site. Clearly, something dreadful had occurred, but exactly what calamity could have precipitated these multiple fires?

For an answer we must turn our attention to RAF Valley, where, after lunch that Thursday, two of the station's sleek Hawker Hunter jets – single seat F.6s XF384 and XF387 – were in the air. Piloting one of the Hunters was an RAF Flight Lieutenant while a 20-year old Officer Cadet of the Royal Jordanian Air Force was flying the second aircraft, though it is not known which pilot was in which machine.

A few minutes before 2.00 p.m. the Jordanian pilot was practising 'roller' landings using Valley's runway 14. He completed a circuit, landed and rolled briefly before taking off once again. Following the normal traffic pattern he climbed to 500 feet, turned left and levelled off at 1,000 feet on the 'live' side of the circuit as he began his downwind leg. Meanwhile, the second Hunter pilot was approaching Valley and requested permission from Air Traffic Control to join the circuit. He was given permission to do so and at the same time given a warning about the presence of other traffic, by which the controller meant the Hunter piloted by the Jordanian student. Then the RAF pilot flew along the 'dead' side of the circuit looking, one presumes, for the other Hunter – which was turning on to its downwind leg – and, failing to see him, decided to join the 'live' circuit there and then. In other words, instead of flying a sufficient distance from the threshold of runway 14 before turning he 'cut the corner' so to speak. But although he failed to spot the Jordanian his 'short cut' had, in fact, put him on a collision course with the second Hunter, which at that moment was proceeding normally on its downwind leg. Unfortunately, the RAF pilot's aircraft was in the Jordanian's blind spot and it was apparent, because neither pilot took any avoiding action, that they had not seen each other.

In the ensuing collision the Jordanian's machine was hit amidships by the other Hunter and cut in half. At the moment of impact the aircraft were one mile from the airfield, flying at a height of 1,000 feet directly above Silver Bay Caravan Park. There were a number of witnesses to the accident, the most important being a holidaymaker on Rhosneigr beach, who filmed the event with his cine camera and whose film proved to be of great value to the subsequent Board of Inquiry. Also, the Squadron Leader who commanded the Hunter squadron at Valley happened to be watching the doomed aircraft from his office window. His reaction is not recorded although his anguish and dismay at what he was seeing can easily be imagined. One witness in the caravan park – a woman from Birmingham – stated that she saw the two jets, which appeared to her to be close to each other. 'Both planes turned together' she said, 'but one seemed to turn more or less into the centre of the other.' A man, sitting outside the Park's cafe drinking tea also witnessed the collision. 'I looked up', he stated, 'and I saw one aircraft going into the other, ripping off a wing.'

The result of the collision was, of course, catastrophic. Both machines disintegrated, allowing burning wreckage to fall on to the unsuspecting caravan park below, with the tragic consequence of the death of the dentist's wife. Others were much luckier than her, however. Two young girls were able to escape from their caravan as the flames enveloped the next van to theirs and wreckage showered around them. A family from Liverpool were sunbathing just outside their caravan when burning debris began to fall, including an engine, which smashed through the roof of their vehicle as if it was made of paper. 'We ran for our lives' remarked a family member tersely. Amongst the remains of the two Hunters lay the bodies of the pilots; the RAF pilot had been killed instantly while the Jordanian had ejected but was too low for his parachute to deploy fully.

After the accident some of Silver Bay's residents decided to cut short their holidays because the stifling pall of death and destruction hanging over the site proved too much for them to bear, especially when the wreckage had to be left *in situ* for crash investigators to examine. But other caravanners were determined to stay on and not let the accident mar their holiday. 'Lightning doesn't strike twice in the same place' said one optimist, the collision 'was a million to one chance' commented another.

Thursday, 10 August 1972 was certainly a black day for both Valley and the Silver Bay Caravan Park whose propinquity to the airfield had brought about such a sudden and unexpected dampening of the site's holiday spirit. For the woman who died, the fickle hand of fate inflicted upon her a cruel end. She had the singularly rare misfortune of losing her life through injuries caused by pieces of a burning, crashing aircraft falling upon her but she was, and remains, singular in another sense also. Hers is the *only* civilian death, to date, in Anglesey and North Wales brought about by an accident involving aircraft from RAF Valley since the start of flying training operations at the base in 1951. Let us hope that this statistical singularity remains unchanged for a long time.

18

Inverted Ejection

In 1976 RAF Valley's long serving Gnat trainers were finally phased out, to be replaced by the British Aerospace Hawk, a much superior aircraft to its predecessor in many respects: vastly improved fuel consumption, simplified maintenance procedures, ease of operation and handling being just a few examples. Safety was also improved at Valley and since the Hawk's introduction into service not a single accident resulting in loss of life occurred until 28 July 1982.

On the morning of that day, a Wednesday, Hawk XX305, in its red and white 'raspberry ripple' livery, had taken off with a Qualified Flying Instructor (QFI) and his student on board, to carry out one of the many exercises necessary to take the student a little further along that hurdle-filled path which led eventually, the student (and everyone connected with his training) hoped, to the award of his 'wings' as a fully fledged pilot. Sadly, that particular distinction would never become a reality for the trainee sitting in the front seat of XX305.

During the course of the flight a noise was heard behind the instructor's seat and almost immediately an unfamiliar odour filled the cockpit. In accordance with standard procedure both pilots switched from their normal oxygen supply to the emergency supply connected to their ejection seats. This source was of limited duration, being available for only ten minutes or so. Then the aircraft's systems and controls were checked for correct functioning. All proved to be working properly, including the engine, which, with rpm and temperatures as they should be, continued to deliver power smoothly and effectively. Yet *something* was amiss, there was no doubt of that, but what could it be?

Neither pilot could discover the puzzling fault, and so,

although the Hawk seemed to be in no immediate danger, good airmanship and common sense dictated that it was wise to abandon the sortie and return to base. This the instructor did.

On the flight back to Valley the aircraft behaved perfectly because, as we now know, there was nothing wrong with its control systems. But in the meantime a secondary problem had arisen. The student complained that he was feeling dizzy, leading the instructor to conclude that his companion in the aircraft was breathing the pressurised oxygen of the emergency supply too quickly, allowing a medical state known as hyperventilation to develop. Sufferers display symptoms of dizziness (as here), blurred vision, numbness of the limbs, mental confusion and in extreme cases, loss of consciousness. The instructor told his student how to overcome dizziness by breathing more slowly, advice which seemed to have the necessary effect but the alleviation of the problem was only temporary. By the time the jet was preparing to land, the student's difficulties had reappeared. With XX305 about to execute its final turn (literally so) to land on runway 14 and with only thirty seconds remaining before touch down, the student once more complained of a problem with his breathing. This distracted the QFI at a critical moment. Instead of concentrating on landing the aircraft, he allowed his natural concern for the well-being of his student to gain the upper hand – a lapse of concentration which, ironically, had fatal results for the student.

When turning to line up with the runway, the QFI made too tight a turn, consequently putting the machine into a stalled condition. Pre-stall buffet gave a warning of what was to come and so as the aircraft stalled and began to spin – an attitude from which it was, of course, impossible to recover at such a low height – the instructor was forced into an instant decision to eject. Unfortunately, successful ejection was prevented by the fact that the doomed jet was by this time rolling. When the student operated his seat's firing mechanism, the Hawk was almost inverted and so the seat's trajectory took it downwards, to disaster, rather than upwards to the safe deployment of the pilot's parachute, as would have happened if the aircraft was on a more even keel. Less than two seconds after ejecting, the young pilot was dead. He had been killed instantly when his seat hit the ground.

Then the instructor ejected and he too was catapulted in the same direction but because the jet's rolling motion was continuous, the downward path of the seat on this occasion was at a different, more oblique angle to the ground than that of the student's seat, thereby lessening the destructive forces generated at the moment of impact to the point where they became non-fatal. This allowed the instructor to survive, although he was seriously injured. The difference between the trajectories taken by the two ejection seats turned out to be the difference between life and death.

Meanwhile, the Hawk continued spinning earthwards and came down on land close to the airfield's boundary, ploughing a 400-yard long furrow between two houses and leaving a trail of wreckage which slightly damaged one of the properties. This house was the holiday home of a Cheshire family, who were in residence that day but shortly before the accident occurred (at midday) they had gone on a shopping trip. When the family returned they were shocked to find the remains of a burnt-out Hawk in their front garden. The whole area had been sealed off and was swarming with policemen, firemen, ambulance crews, RAF officers and airmen, their vehicles blocking the narrow roads while helicopters buzzed overhead.

Within hours a Board of Inquiry had been set up to investigate the crash but it soon became evident that the investigation was going to be a protracted affair and would take many months to complete. In fact, the inquest into the death of the student pilot was delayed for over a year by the lengthy nature of the Board's probings and was not held until November 1983, sixteen months after the accident. It was at this inquest that the root cause of the Hawk's problems was revealed by the RAF; nothing more serious than the failure of the aircraft's air conditioning system. No threat was posed to the integrity of the airframe or its airworthiness by this failure, no emergency would have arisen if the flight had continued and the net effect of the failure would, possibly, have been little more than an increased degree of personal discomfort for the two pilots. Yet, it is unarguable that the instructor acted correctly in returning to base but wholly unfortunate that his student experienced the effects of hyperventilation when he switched to his emergency oxygen supply.

As noted already, this supply, because it is restricted in its usage, is only of limited duration. By the time the jet trainer was about to land, the student's oxygen was running out, hence the recurrence of his breathing difficulties. However, as a member of the Board of Inquiry told the inquest, all the student pilot had to do was switch back to the aircraft's main supply and the problem would have been solved.

During subsequent years a number of other Hawk crashes took place, some fatal, others not. For example, two men were killed when XX166 flew into high ground on the Isle of Man in June 1983, XX298 was lost in the sea off Harlech in October 1994, a mid-air collision occurred between XX182 and XX291 near Machynlleth in June 1989, killing one of the pilots, XX347 crashed near Valley in May 1990 after the pilot ejected safely, XX288 was practising 'roller' landings at RAF Mona during August 1995 when the Royal Navy student pilot lost control and ejected, leaving the aircraft to its fate – a destructive crash followed by an even more destructive fire. In April 1998 XX186 was abandoned at a height of 7,500 feet over the Irish Sea some fifteen miles west of Valley when the crew experienced control problems and had no alternative but to eject. They were picked up twenty-five minutes after ejecting by their SAR colleagues from Valley and were found to be injured though their injuries were not life-threatening. The aircraft had been part of a three-ship group engaged in air to air combat exercises.

Strangely enough, the latest fatality to have occurred at the time of writing (November 1999) bears a tragic resemblance to the first, whose details have been recounted in the preceding few pages. At 7.45 a.m. on Tuesday, 13 February 1996 a 28-year old QFI at Valley climbed into the front cockpit of Hawk XX164 and prepared to take off. The man was a highly experienced aviator who, five years previously had taken part, as a Tornado pilot, in the Gulf War but was unlucky enough to be taken prisoner by the Iraqis. His period of captivity, lasting forty-one days, became a harrowing ordeal of beatings, torture and death threats at gunpoint. However, by 1996 such distressing experiences were half a decade in the past and the pilot's duty that February morning was straightforward and routine; to fly the so-called 'weather ship', a relatively brief sortie to check weather conditions in the immediate area before any of Valley's students took to the air. Everything had been perfectly normal with the start-up, taxying and take-off run of the Hawk up to the moment at which unstick speed was reached, when, only a few seconds after becoming airborne, the aircraft's flight ended in catastrophe.

Observers in the control tower watched the jet accelerate along Valley's main runway, saw the machine leave the ground and gain forty feet of height before starting to roll to starboard. At 100 feet the aircraft stopped climbing and the pilot was seen to eject, but as in the case of the hyperventilating student, he did so when the Hawk was not level – it was at an angle of ninety degrees. Thus, instead of firing upwards, the ejection seat cannoned its occupant sideways and downwards, and as before, the result was the same; a violent collision with the ground, killing the pilot instantly. His aircraft remained airborne briefly before veering off the runway and crashing on the airfield. The flight had lasted twelve seconds only.

The question was what could have caused an experienced pilot to lose control of the Hawk immediately it became airborne? Rumours soon began to circulate that a maintenance error was to blame for the crash. The jet's ailerons were disconnected, it was said, during maintenance and had not been reconnected to the control system when XX164 was returned to the flight line. At the time, the RAF was refusing to confirm or deny this, but *Flight International*, that most authoritative of aviation journals stated (in the edition dated 13-19 March 1996) that;

> The British Aerospace Hawk which crashed at the Royal Air Force training base at Valley, North Wales, in February took off with its ailerons disconnected after maintenance. This was one of a series of human errors contributing to the crash, according to initial investigations . . . The RAF declines to comment . . . As part of the pre-flight checks, correct control-surface input and movement should also have been visually confirmed by the pilot and groundcrew. The pilot would have been unable to tell from stick feel that the ailerons were disconnected. The [inital RAF accident] bulletin re-stressed that aircrew must make sure that all control surfaces move correctly as part of the pre-flight checks.'

The magazine's editorial comment was rather censorious in its tone, particularly of the RAF's political masters;

> [The accident] reveals a tragic and disturbing litany of human error. Taken on its own, this fatal crash should strongly focus minds on how to improve safety. Placed in the context of a series of losses [the RAF lost more aircraft in the first two months of 1996 than during the whole of 1995] it raises nagging doubts that this is not simply a single, avoidable incident, but early warning of a widespread malaise in the service.
>
> In recent years [the RAF's] political masters have tasked it to do a great deal . . . The service is being asked to balance an increasingly unmanageable equation of doing more and more, or at least the same, with considerably less resource. The point is being reached when politicians will have to re-

examine the demands placed upon the junior service. The aircraft losses in general and the Hawk crash in particular, should be a wake up call to all those involved.

Exactly a year after the crash, the inquest was held. It confirmed what *Flight International* had already said in March 1996; the Hawk's ailerons were indeed disconnected when the jet became airborne. On the night before the acccident a servicing team which should have consisted of eleven men was down to six, and of those only two had much previous experience of the Hawk. The team was very busy that night, with a dozen aircraft to attend to, including XX164. It was expected of the technicians that whatever the pressure of work upon them, they would get the jets into a serviceable condition, but unfortunately, in the case of XX164 a rod in the aileron control linkage was disconnected and left in this state without the error being spotted. When rolled out on to the flight line on the morning of the 13th, the Hawk was far from being serviceable. It was, in fact, a highly dangerous machine.

But how was it that checks failed to uncover the flaw in the control system? The NCO in charge of the maintenance team was close to the truth when he said that in his opinion, 'the fatal error had been due to undermanning' – a point made by *Flight International* in its castigatory editorial. On the day after the NCO spoke these words, the *Guardian* (13 February 1997) printed an article whose message was that funding cutbacks and manpower shortages were beginning to make serious inroads into the RAF's operational efficiency. The writer of the article had been given a preview of a television programme to be transmitted on Channel 4 that evening. Entitled *Crash Landing*, the programme was another in the *Dispatches* investigative journalism series. For anyone concerned with flight safety *Crash Landing* was not enjoyable viewing. Although the programme's reporter, David Lomax, had been denied access to RAF stations and the MoD had informed RAF personnel not to cooperate with him, Lomax had, nevertheless, in the way that hard-nosed journalists always seem to overcome impediments put in their path, put together a film which told a tragic tale of aircraft servicing mistakes leading to loss of life.

Many a friend of RAF Valley must have winced at this programme. The airfield was prominently featured, especially the crash of Hawk XX164, the inquest into which, having taken place the previous day, was therefore fresh and so the transmission date of *Dispatches* on the 13th, only twenty-four hours after the inquest, was most opportune but whether this coincidence came about through pure chance or was deliberately contrived to maximise the impact of the film is not known, though one can hazard a guess that the latter was probably the case. The programme catalogued a series of alleged failures and linked the rise in accidents with the relentless cutbacks. 'A proud service heading for a crash landing . . . the 1996 safety record was the worst for five years . . . corner cutting is putting [the RAF] in the dock . . . the RAF is being asked to do more and more with less and less' were some of the statements made in the film.

As regards Hawk XX164, some interesting discoveries were made by the programme's sleuthing researchers. Five weeks before the accident, aircrew at Valley complained to the engineers that too many aircraft were being declared serviceable and put on the Flight Line but with potentially serious faults. Two weeks later, the same complaint was made and three weeks after that, the Hawk crashed. There were reports of undermanning in the Engineering Wing – only thirteen technicians out of an establishment of twenty-three were on the night shift before the accident (a point also raised at the inquest). Additionally, mention was made of shortcuts in paperwork and lax procedures. These claims were borne out by quotes from the RAF's own report into the crash, which spoke of, 'The common practice of not raising paperwork for "trivial" tasks, thereby acting as a catalyst to escalate that practice to an unacceptable level.' The report then went on to remark on one hapless technician's 'failure to raise paperwork for tasks that he considered minor, which included disturbance of flying controls.' The supervising NCO that night did not know XX164's ailerons had been disconnected. When he signed the Form 700, handing the aircraft over to the pilot as being in an airworthy condition, the very opposite was the case.

Two years after the accident, the unfortunate technician was court martialled on a charge of neglect leading to the death of a pilot. The charge alleged that the 33-year old airman, whilst servicing Hawk XX164, disconnected an aileron control rod and then 'negligently carried out his duty as to fail to make an entry on an appropriate form, which caused the loss of life of [the pilot] when he later flew the aircraft.' The technician pleaded Not Guilty to the charge against him, blaming understaffing and overwork for his mistake, but after all the evidence had been heard he was found guilty and ordered to be dismissed from the Service. Additionally, he was fined £2,000. In an expression of charitableness the parents of the deceased pilot said they did not feel any personal animosity towards the disgraced technician. Rather, their anger was directed more towards the government, which had imposed financial restraints upon the armed forces. 'RAF cutbacks killed our son' was the headline in a local newspaper reporting the proceedings of the court martial.

How then, in the light of *Dispatches* and the outcome of the technician's trial, should the Hawk's loss be viewed? Was the crash just another unfortunate incident or was it indicative of a worrying trend within the RAF? The strictures of *Flight International* are plain enough, but let us be fair to the RAF technicians and pilots. If we likened them to the branches of a tree and its trunk the military bosses, the Air Marshals and Chiefs of Staff, then the tree's roots were the politicians determining Defence policy and it was their undisguised desire to see budget savings effected as quickly as possible that was at the heart of the problem.

While most would agree that the armed forces could not remain as they were during the Cold War and that economies had to be made once that conflict was over, the cuts applied to the RAF in particular were, in the words of one Air Vice Marshal interviewed for *Dispatches*, 'too fast, short term and in the end counter-productive'. The word that comes to mind here is downsizing – that 1980s and 1990s euphemism for reducing the number of employees in an organisation without necessarily reducing the work. As a process, downsizing and the philosophy which underpins it has limits when applied to the RAF, especially where flight safety is concerned. Endless financial constraints and manpower cutbacks, however laudible from a management (that is, government and MoD) point of view, are not acceptable when set against the loss of pilot's lives. If anyone doubts this, then let them ask the grieving families of those pilots who have died.

Appendix

Flying Accidents in Anglesey, 1910-1999
(The list is not definitive. Minor incidents have been omitted)

Date	Aircraft	Location	Remarks
12 August 1910	Farman Biplane	Llanfairynghornwy	Hit hummock on take off. First crash in Anglesey.
4 September 1910	Farman Biplane	Llanfairynghornwy	Failed to take off and crashed.
7 November 1917	Airco DH4 A7654	RNAS Station Mona	Crashed on landing. First fatal accident in Anglesey.
18 April 1919	Short Shirl, N111 *Shamrock*	In the sea off Holyhead	Ditched during attempt on Atlantic crossing.
18 April 1919	Short Shirl, N112	Holyhead	Accompanying *Shamrock*. Hit stone wall on landing. Pilot unhurt.

Date	Aircraft	Location	Notes
September 1930	Avro 504K G-ABAV	Holyhead	Belonged to Northern Air Transport Ltd.
5 February 1940	Saro London K6927	Holyhead harbour	From 240 Squadron, Sullom Voe Emergency landing in bad weather. Aircraft broke its back but all 11 occupants survived.
4 March 1940	Bristol Blenheim L1185	Aberffraw	From RAF Bicester. Forced landing due to bad weather.
10 June 1940	Hawker Henley L3432	In the sea off Rhosneigr	From RAF Penrhos. Struck the water after low flying in bad weather. Two killed.
6 July 1940	Hawker Henley L3418	Malltraeth Bay	Dived into the sea. Both crewmen killed.
9 October 1940	Avro Anson K6274	RAF Bodorgan	From RAF Squires Gate. Force landed on obstructed part of the airfield. Aircraft damaged.
11 October 1940	Dornier Do 17 7T+EH	In the sea off Carmel Head	Shot down by pilots of 611 Squadron, RAF Tern Hill.

29 November 1940	Avro Anson N9742	In the sea off Holyhead	From 321 Squadron. Aircraft ditched.
21 December 1940	Hawker Hurricane V7023	Bodorgan	From 79 Squadron, RAF Pembrey. Crashed on beach during forced landing.
13 March 1941	Supermarine Spitfire L1034	Beaumaris	From RAF Hawarden. Crashed on houses. No fatalities or injuries.
6 May 1941	Blackburn Botha L6265	In the sea near Puffin Island	Crashed in the sea. One crewman drowned.
13 May 1941	Hawker Hurricane V6551	In the sea off Holyhead	From 615 Sq., Valley. Ditched after engine trouble. Pilot was seen in the water but disappeared before he could be rescued.
15 May 1941	Hawker Hurricane V6788	Rhoscolyn	From RAF Valley. Crashed on beach, pilot seriously injured.

1 July 1941	Bristol Blenheim P6896	RAF Valley	From 56 OTU. Crashed on take-off.
21 July 1941	Boulton Paul Defiant T3933	Llanerchymedd	From RAF Valley. Stalled and spun in. Pilot killed.
4 August 1941	Hawker Hurricane Z2404	Dwyran	From 615 Squadron, Valley.
16 August 1941	Hawker Hurricane Z2578	Llanddeusant	From 615 Squadron, Valley. Crashed in flames, pilot killed.
26 August 1941	Supermarine Spitfire R7228	RAF Valley	From 72 Squadron. Wheels raised during take-off. Crashed one mile from the airfield.
28 August 1941	Blackburn Botha L6417	In the sea off Rhosneigr	Failed to take off from Valley and came down in the sea 500 yards from shore. Failed rescue attempts resulted in the drowning of eleven rescuers and two crew members.

15 September 1941	Bristol Blenheim V5567	Bodorgan	From 236 Squadron. Ran out of fuel and abandoned by its crew of three. One was drowned.
17 September 1941	Bristol Blenheim T2352	RAF Valley	Crashed on take off.
17 September 1941	Supermarine Spitfire X4789	Newborough	From 132 Squadron. Engine failed, after which the pilot made a wheels-up landing.
1 November 1941	Heinkel He 111 F8+KR	Bodffordd	Shot down by P/O Shipard of 68 Squadron.
13 November 1941	Avro Anson N9532	In the sea off Bodorgan	From RAF Penrhos. Forced to ditch in bad weather.
15 November 1941	Bristol Beaufighter T3024	RAF Valley	From 456 Sq., Valley. Struck sand dunes on landing and broke off undercarriage.
18 November 1941	Bristol Beaufighter R2334	RAF Valley	Crashed on landing. Aircraft written off.

Date	Aircraft	Location	Remarks
20 November 1941	Bristol Beaufighter R2372	RAF Valley	From 456 Sq., Valley. Swung to port on landing and undercarriage broken off.
24 November 1941	Supermarine Spitfires P8661 P7284	Llanfair P.G. RAF Valley	On delivery flight to Valley in bad weather. Pilot of P8661 killed, other pilot unhurt.
5 January 1942 (16.45 hours)	Bristol Beaufighter R2474	Rhosneigr	From 456 Sq., Valley. Both crewmen killed.
(19.55 hours)	Bristol Beaufighter T3028	RAF Valley	From 456 Sq., Valley. Struck glide path indicator.
(20.55 hours)	Bristol Beaufighter R2476	RAF Valley	From 456 Sq., Valley. Force landed one mile from base after flap failure. Crew unhurt but aircraft written off.
8 January 1942	Supermarine Spitfire P8702 Westland Lysander	RAF Valley Trewan Sands	Mid-air collision. Lysander spun in and pilot killed. Spitfire crashed and pilot injured.

26 January 1942	Hawker Sea Hurricane P3452	In the sea off Red Wharf Bay	Pilot abandoned aircraft but drowned. He was the winner of the 1929 Grand National.
28 January 1942	Bristol Beaufighter T3047	RAF Valley	From 456 Sq., Valley. Undershot during night landing, undercarriage collapsed and aircraft hit a sand dune.
30 January 1942	Bristol Beaufighter T3026	RAF Valley	From 456 Sq., Valley.Landed with its undercarriage up.
20 March 1942	Bristol Beaufighter T3012	RAF Valley	From 456 Sq., Valley. Hit windsock and burst into flames.
23 March 1942	Supermarine Spitfire BL411 & Spitfire, serial no. unknown	RAF Valley	From 131 Sq., Valley. Mid-air collision. BL411 crashed and other Spitfire force landed. Both pilots survived.
28 April 1942	Hawker Henley L3366	RAF Bodorgan	Crashed on final approach.

Date	Aircraft	Location	Details
30 April 1942	Vickers Wellington DV442	South Stack, Holyhead	From 15 OTU. Failed ditching. Three crewmen drowned and three survived.
2 May 1942	Bristol Beaufighter R2381	RAF Valley	From 456 Sq., Valley. Crashed on take off. Crew survived.
9 May 1942	de Havilland Tiger Moth T5491	RAF Bodorgan	Crashed on landing.
30 May 1942	Blackburn Botha W5088	Llanddwyn Island	From 48 MU. Pilot slightly injured. Passenger drowned.
8 June 1942	Hawker Henley L3352	Near the shore at Bodorgan	From RAF Bodorgan. After an engine fire near Bardsey the aircraft attempted to reach base but was forced to ditch. Both crewmen safe.
28 July 1942	Lockheed Lightning P-38	RAF Valley	Crashed on take off but pilot unhurt.

Date	Aircraft	Location	Details
6 August 1942	Avro Anson AX408	Malltraeth Sands	From No.3 (O)AFU. Crashed during forced landing.
20 August 1942	Vickers Wellington Z1172	In the sea off South Stack, Holyhead	From 304 Squadron, RAF Dale. No survivors from a six-man Polish crew.
14 September 1942	Bristol Beaufighter X8205	Penmynydd	Force landed with engine trouble. Minor injuries to crew. Aircraft caught fire and burnt out.
26 September 1942	Hawker Henley L3301	Tŷ Croes	From RAF Bodorgan. Hit gun position after 'beat-up'. Both crewmen killed.
8 October 1942	Bristol Beaufighter X8190	Newborough Warren 'Q' Site	From 456 Sq., Valley. Landed on decoy runway at night. Two crewmen killed.
16 October 1942	Bristol Beaufighter X8206	RAF Valley	From 456 Sq., Valley. Aircraft stalled on to runway. Slight injuries to pilot.

30 November 1942	de Havilland Tiger Moth DE425	RAF Bodorgan	Crash landing. Aircraft written off.
10 January 1943	Bristol Beaufighter X8194	Cemaes Bay	From 456 Sq., Valley. Crash landed after hitting house during cine-gun attacks on ground targets. Pilot unhurt.
25 January 1943	de Havilland Mosquito DZ658	RAF Valley	From 456 Sq. Undershot at night and hit the ground. Crew unhurt.
1 February 1943	Handley Page Halifax BB275	Four Mile Bridge	From 1659 HCU. Engine failure followed by fuel system mismanagement. No survivors.
11 February 1943	Hawker Henley	Malltraeth Bay	From RAF Bodorgan. Ditched due to engine failure. Crew unhurt.
15 February 1943	Blackburn Botha W5029	RAF Mona	From Mona. Crashed on landing and aircraft badly damaged.

Date	Aircraft	Location	Details
28 February 1943	Blackburn Botha W5024	RAF Mona	From Mona. Crashed on landing and aircraft badly damaged.
29 March 1943	Avro Anson DJ618	In the sea off Holyhead	From RAF Llandwrog. Ditched but crew in the sea for six hours and were rescued suffering from exposure.
4 April 1943	Miles Martinet HP267	RAF Valley	From Valley. Force landed after engine failure. Crew slightly hurt.
7 May 1943	Supermarine Walrus R6590	In the sea off Cemlyn Bay	From 275 Sq., Valley. Practising sea landings. Got into difficulties and sank. Crew rescued.
14 May 1943	Blackburn Botha L6373 & Avro Anson LT528	RAF Mona	Botha collided with Anson on landing. Former written off but latter aircraft repairable.
17 May 1943	Blackburn Botha L6419	RAF Mona	From RAF Mona. Crashed on landing. Aircraft written off.

22 June 1943	Avro Anson LT338	Llangwyllog	From RAF Mona. Force landed due to engine trouble. Aircraft badly damaged.
19 July 1943	Vickers Wellington DV455	Near Bodedern	From No.28 OTU. Crashed on a car, burning three occupants to death.
3 August 1943	Handley Page Halifax JB916	In the sea off Rhoscolyn	From 1659 HCU. Ditched and all seven crew rescued.
11 August 1943	Bristol Beaufighter X7966	RAF Valley	From Valley. Swung on take off and undercarriage collapsed.
20 August 1943	de Havilland Mosquito DZ714	RAF Valley	From RAF High Ercall. Crashed in the sea after emergency landing. Crew safe.
21 August 1943	Avro Anson LT146	In the sea off Point Lynas	From SPTU. Ditched on night navex. Crew rescued safely by motor launch.
18 October 1943	Bristol Beaufighter V8717	Tŷ Croes	From 406 Sq., Valley. Broke up in mid-air. Pilot killed.

Date	Aircraft	Location	Details
21 October 1943	Armstrong Whitworth Whitley Z9490	In the sea off Moelfre	From No.42 OTU, RAF Ashbourne. Ditched after engine failure. Crew rescued by Moelfre lifeboat.
9 November 1943	de Havilland Tiger Moth T7612	Llangaffo	From RAF Bodorgan. Unauthorised low flying. Both crewmen killed.
10 November 1943	Handley Page Halifax EB157	In the sea off Holyhead	From 1664 HCU. Descended through cloud and struck the water. All crew survived.
22 November 1943	Bristol Beaufighter T5318	In the sea off Holyhead	From No.9 OTU. Ditched. Two crewmen drowned.
11 December 1943	Supermarine Seafire	Cable Bay	From RNAS St.Merryn. Force landed and pilot suffered slight injury.
15 January 1944	Avro Anson MG627	Tynygongl	From RAF Llandwrog. Aircraft badly damaged after forced landing.

29 January 1944	Avro Anson EG609	Llanerchymedd	From RAF Mona. Of five crew members, one was killed, three seriously injured and one slightly injured.
8 February 1944	Miles Martinet HP183	Gorsgoch, Holyhead	From RAF Bodorgan. 'Beat up' of gun emplacement. Pilot killed.
11 February 1944	Miles Martinet MS784 and de Havilland Mosquito HK752	near Tŷ Croes Army Camp	The Mosquito collided with a drogue towed by the Martinet and lost seven feet from its starboard wing but still landed safely at Valley.
20 February 1944	Bristol Beaufighter JL616	RAF Valley	From RAF Crosby. Crashed during emergency landing. Crew killed instantly.
3 March 1944	Blackburn Botha L6488	In the sea near the Skerries	From No.11 Radio School, RAF Hooton Park. Of 4 crew, 2 were lost and 2 rescued by motor launch.

Date	Aircraft	Location	Details
25 March 1944	Avro Anson DJ315	Rhydwyn	From RAF Llandwrog. Hit high ground while descending through cloud. Crew unhurt.
12 April 1944	de Havilland Tiger Moth N9161	Bodedern	Piloted by Station Commander, RAF Bodorgan. Both pilot and passenger seriously injured.
23 July 1944	Vickers Wellington MF654	RAF Valley	From No.27 OTU. Landed with port engine u/s and without flaps. Touched down at 130 mph and crashed beyond runway 14.
2 September 1944	Douglas Dakota	RAF Valley	Crash landed with one engine on fire. Crew unhurt but aircraft destroyed.
26 November 1944	Vickers Wellington	RAF Valley	Diverted from RAF Bramcote. Crashed on landing and aircraft badly damaged. Crew unhurt.
18 December 1944	Avro Anson EG218	RAF Valley	From RAF Llandwrog. Belly landed near domestic site after engine failure.

22 December 1944	Consolidated Liberator 42-51232 *the Jigs Up*	In the sea off North Stack, Holyhead	Diverted from Cheddington to Valley but ran out of fuel before landing. Of ten crewmen eight drowned and two survived.
8 February 1945	Avro Ansons EG390 & NK678	RAF Mona	Ground collision on perimeter track.
14 February 1945	Avro Anson AX180	Llanerchymedd	From RAF Squires Gate. Port engine failed and pilot force landed in a field.
16 May 1945	Avro Anson N9911	RAF Mona	From RAF Llandwrog. Crashed during night landing. Three crew killed and one injured.
20 June 1945	North American Mustang P.51	RAF Valley	From 356 Fighter Group, Martlesham Heath. Caught in severe thunderstorm and crashed in the sea near Valley. Pilot killed.

27 July 1945	Airspeed Oxford PH394	Caergeiliog	From Valley. Emergency landing due to engine trouble. Aircraft badly damaged.
6 August 1945	Douglas A26 Invader	RAF Valley	Crashed on final approach. Aircraft destroyed but pilot unhurt.
7 June 1951	de Havilland Vampire FB5 VX333	RAF Valley	From Valley. Hit the ground on final approach and lost its undercarriage. Pilot unhurt.
2 July 1951	de Havilland Vampire FB5 WA298	In the sea near Llanddwyn	From Valley. Crashed on instrument let-down, probably due to inadvertent dinghy inflation. Persian pilot killed.
5 July 1951	Supermarine Spitfire TE344	Bodedern	From 20 Squadron. Crashed during forced landing.
31 July 1951	de Havilland Vampire FB5 WA160	Dulas Bay	From Valley. Hit water whilst low flying. Believed to be the first successful ditching of a Vampire.

Date	Aircraft	Location	Details
4 December 1951	Gloster Meteor T.7 WF777	Silver Bay, Rhoscolyn	From Valley. Forced landing after one engine inadvertently cut by pupil pilot. Aircraft badly damaged but occupants unhurt.
21 December 1951	Gloster Meteor T.7 WA716	Malltraeth Marsh	From Valley. Ran out of fuel and crashed during forced landing.
21 December 1951	de Havilland Vampire FB5 VV547	RAF Valley	From Valley. Brake failure after landing. The pilot selected undercarriage 'up' to avoid an overshoot.
6 March 1952	de Havilland Vampires FB5 VV446 & WA290	RAF Valley	Collided during formation take off.
1 May 1952	de Havilland Vampire FB5 WA426	Bryngwran, near Treban Crossroads	From Valley. Crashed during forced landing. The pilot survived.

13 August 1952	de Havilland Vampire FB5 WA418	RAF Valley	From Valley. Crashed during final approach. Pilot badly injured.
24 November 1952	de Havilland Vampire FB5 VZ863	Llynfaes	From Valley. Aircraft in spin. Pilot parachuted to safety.
19 March 1953	de Havilland Vampire FB5 WE835	RAF Valley	From Valley. Overshot during emergency landing and pilot killed.
8 April 1953	Gloster Meteor T.7 WF857	RAF Valley	From Valley. Hit ground when avoiding collision with Vampire on approach.
19 May 1953	Hawker Sea Furies F-25 & F-28	Rhydwyn	From the Dutch Navy. Mid-air collision in bad weather with third Sea Fury, F-43. Two pilots killed.

9 July 1953	de Havilland Vampire FB5 WA134	Llanerchymedd	From Valley. Abandoned in inverted spin but pilot killed when his parachute failed to open.
24 October 1953	de Havilland Vampire FB5 VV226	Near the Skerries	From Valley. Engine flame out followed by failed ditching.
11 December 1953	de Havilland Vampire FB5 WA459	Tŷ Croes	From Valley. Engine failure after taking off.
7 January 1954	de Havilland Vampire T.11 WZ561	Pentraeth	From Valley. Spun in and the two occupants were killed.
27 February 1954	de Havilland Vampire FB5 VZ206	RAF Valley	From Valley. Crash landed.
16 July 1954	de Havilland Vampire FB5 WA307	RAF Mona	From Valley. Crashed during unauthorised low level aerobatics. Pilot killed.

Date	Aircraft	Location	Details
16 November 1954	de Havilland Vampire FB5 VV659	Rhoscolyn	From Valley. Abandoned in spin. Pilot rescued by DUKW.
13 December 1954	de Havilland Vampire FB5 VZ128	RAF Valley	From Valley. Crash landed and damaged beyond repair.
5 January 1955	Gloster Meteor F.8 WA788	RAF Valley	From the Royal Aircraft Establishment. Crashed on landing.
8 December 1955	de Havilland Vampire T.11 XD591	RAF Mona	From Valley. Lost power on take-off and overshot. Pilot retracted undercarriage to stop.
31 December 1955	de Havilland Vampire FB5 VV554	Llangefni	From Valley. Pilot killed.
23 June 1956	de Havilland Vampire FB5 WA285	In the sea off Holyhead	From Valley. Aircraft abandoned after engine failure.

28 September 1956	de Havilland Vampire FB5 WG845	RAF Valley	From Valley. Engine failure after take off. Pilot killed.
29 January 1957	de Havilland Vampire FB5 WG835	RAF Valley	From Valley. Lost power on take-off and overshot across road into lake. Pilot unhurt.
10 April 1957	de Havilland Vampire T.11 XH319	RAF Valley	From Valley. Severe birdstrike. Aircraft badly damaged.
12 December 1957	de Havilland Vampire FB9 WP993	Marianglas	From Valley. Pilot lost control during aerobatics and was killed.
3 February 1958	Hawker Sea Hawk	RAF Valley	Royal Navy aircraft. Stalled during landing and crashed. Pilot killed.
22 December 1958	de Havilland Vampire FB9 WR137	Gwaenydog, Rhosgoch	From Valley. Aircraft caught fire and dived into the ground. Pilot killed.

Date	Aircraft	Location	Notes
24 April 1961	de Havilland Vampire T.11 XK584	Llanddeusant	From Valley. Abandoned in a spin by two occupants.
18 July 1961	de Havilland Chipmunk T.10 WG319	RAF Valley	From Oxford University Air Squadron. Hit obstruction on ground and damaged beyond repair.
8 August 1962	de Havilland Vampire T.11 XD620	Rhostrehwfa	From Valley. Crashed into a cottage. Pilot killed.
24 April 1963	de Havilland Vampire T.11 WZ612	RAF Valley	From Valley. Undercarriage collapsed on landing. Last Vampire accident in Anglesey.
25 November 1963	Westland Whirlwind HAR10 helicopter XD164	Holyhead	From CFS. Ditched offshore after engine failure.
10 December 1963	Hawker Siddeley Gnat T.1 XP542	RAF Valley	Landed with nose wheel up.

Date	Aircraft	Location	Notes
16 July 1964	Avro Vulcan B.1 XA909	Gwalchmai	From 101 Squadron. All five crew members successfully baled out.
12 October 1964	Hawker Siddeley Gnat T.1 XR976	Rhosneigr	From Valley. Two pilots ejected safely.
14 January 1965	Hawker Siddeley Gnat T.1 XR568	RAF Valley.	From Valley. Undershot and crashed near runway 32.
9 March 1965	Hawker Siddeley Gnat T.1 XR542	RAF Valley	From Valley. Crashed after engine trouble on approach.
5 April 1965	Hawker Siddeley Gnat T.1 XR985	RAF Valley	From Valley. Badly damaged after heavy landing.
22 April 1965	Hawker Siddeley Gnat T.1 XS108	RAF Valley	From Valley. After mid-air collision with Gnat XR950 near Caernarfon XS108 crashed on landing at Valley. Pilot killed.
19 July 1965	Hawker Siddeley Gnat T.1 XR543	Maelog Lake, Rhosneigr	From Valley. Aircraft stalled on approach. Pilot killed.

6 September 1965	Hawker Siddeley Gnat T.1 XR979	RAF Valley	From Valley. Crashed moments after taking off. Pilot escaped unhurt but the aircraft was badly damaged by fire.
13 April 1966	Hawker Siddeley Gnat T.1 XP507	Cymyran Beach, RAF Valley	From Valley. Crashed on approach. Two killed.
23 August 1967	Hawker Siddeley Gnat T.1 XP512	Rhosneigr beach	From Valley. Abandoned by its crew after experiencing control difficulties.
14 December 1967	Hawker Siddeley Gnat T.1 XP509	RAF Valley	Belly landed and struck off charge.
15 August 1969	Hawker Hunter F.6 XG204	Porth Castell, Cable Bay	From Valley. Flown into the ground after take off. Cause obscure. Pilot killed.
26 November 1969	Westland Whirlwind HAR10 helicopter XP343	RAF Valley	From CFS. Crashed on take off when rotor hit roof. One crewman slightly hurt.

Date	Aircraft	Location	Details
3 January 1970	Hawker Siddeley Gnat T.1 XR997	Llanfaelog	From Valley. Crashed shortly after take off. Both occupants killed.
10 August 1972	Hawker Hunters F.6 XF384 and XF387	Rhoscolyn	From Valley. Mid-air collision. Two pilots and one civilian killed.
13 December 1972	Westland Whirlwind HAR10 helicopter XP349	Holyhead harbour	From Valley. Ditched after engine failure.
5 July 1973	Beagle Basset XS783	Tŷ Croes	From RAF Wyton. Crashed soon after take off. One crewman fatally injured. Aircraft had been refuelled with Avtur instead of Avgas.
6 September 1973	Hawker Siddeley Gnat T.1 XP508	In the sea off Rhoscolyn	From Valley. Aircraft abandoned after engine failure. Pilot ejected but was drowned.
28 October 1975	Hawker Siddeley Gnat T.1 XR571	RAF Valley	From Valley. Damaged beyond repair after PIO during landing.

21 April 1976	Hawker Hunter F.6 XG185	Llanddwyn	From Valley. Pilot parachuted into the sea after aircraft developed engine trouble.
7 February 1978	Hawker Siddeley Gnat T.1 XR541	RAF Mona	From Valley. Barrier engagement. Aircraft written off but crew unhurt.
26 April 1978	Hawker Siddeley Gnat T.1 XR544	Cymyran beach, RAF Valley	From Valley. Crashed after control difficulties experienced. Two occupants ejected safely.
25 August 1978	Beechcraft D95A G-ASIR	Holyhead	On flight to Birmingham from the Isle of Man when engine failed. Five occupants escaped with cuts and bruises.
20 September 1978	Westland Wessex helicopter XP143	In the sea off Holyhead	From 737 Sq., Royal Navy. Ditched 15 miles off Holyhead. Four crew rescued.
25 September 1978	Socata Rallye 150 ST, G-BFBT	Llanfachraeth	Collided with tree during take off. Damaged beyond repair.

Date	Aircraft	Location	Details
17 August 1979	B.A.C. Lightning F3 XP737	RAF Valley	From No.5 Squadron. Suffered hydraulic failure and pilot ejected. Aircraft fell into the sea.
25 October 1979	Hughes 269C light helicopter G-BBIU	Rhosgoch	Engaged on oil pipeline inspection. Collided with power cables. Two men killed.
28 July 1982	B.Ae. Hawk XX305	RAF Valley	From Valley. Crashed during emergency landing. One pilot killed, other seriously injured.
7 November 1984	B.Ae. Hawk XX180	Bodffordd	From Valley. Practising 'roller' landings at RAF Mona when aircraft suffered a birdstrike.
10 May 1985	Socata TB.9 Tampico G-BIAA	RAF Mona	Heavy landing causing extensive damage to aircraft.
7 July 1986	B.Ae. Hawk XX223	RAF Valley	From Valley. Tyre burst during landing. Aircraft ran off runway and crashed.

Date	Aircraft	Location	Details
2 September 1987	Westland Gazelle helicopter ZB627	Aberffraw Common	From RAF Shawbury. Suffered birdstrike. Pilot had cuts and bruises but made a safe landing.
9 May 1990	B.Ae. Hawk XX347	Cymyran beach, RAF Valley	From Valley. Pilot ejected safely.
1 July 1993	B.Ae. Hawk XX163	RAF Valley	From Valley. Both crew ejected safely.
3 October 1993	Jodel D.112 G-BHFF	RAF Mona	Engine started without pilot on board. Aircraft became a runaway, collided with the control tower and was severely damaged.
10 August 1995	B.Ae. Hawk XX288	RAF Mona	From Valley. Pilot lost control during 'roller' landing and ejected. Aircraft destroyed by fire.
13 February 1996	B.Ae. Hawk XX164	RAF Valley	From Valley. Ailerons disconnected and crashed on take off. Pilot killed.

| 30 April 1998 | B.Ae Hawk XX186 | In the sea fifteen miles off Valley | From Valley. Part of 3-ship group. Crew ejected but were injured, though not seriously. |
| 24 August 1999 | B.Ae. Hawk XX160 | RAF Mona | From Valley. Suffered birdstrike on runway. After a barrier engagement the aircraft went into the boundary hedge but suffered minimal damage. |

Bibliography

Alexander, Raymond, *101 Squadron*, published privately by the author, 1979

Bennett, John, *Fighter Nights – 456 Squadron*, Banner Books, Australia, 1995

Hutton, Stephen, *Squadron of Deception – The 36th Bomb Squadron in World War II*, Schiffer Publishing Ltd., USA, 1999

Hywel, William, *Modest Millionaire*, Gwasg Gee, Denbigh, 1973

Loraine, Winifred, *Robert Loraine, Soldier, Actor, Airman*, Collins, 1938

Pratt, Derrick and Grant, Mike, *Wings Across the Border*, Bridge Books, Wrexham, 1998

Sloan, Roy, *Early Aviation in North Wales*, Gwasg Carreg Gwalch, Llanrwst, 1989

Sloan, Roy, *Wings of War over Gwynedd*, Gwasg Carreg Gwalch, Llanrwst, 1991

Sloan, Roy, *Aircraft Crashes in Gwynedd 1910-1999*, Gwasg Carreg Gwalch, Llanrwst, 1994

Sloan, Roy, *Anglesey Airfields during the Second World War*, Transactions of the Anglesey Antiquarian Society, 1995

Sloan, Roy, *Anglesey's First Aviators*, Transactions of the Anglesey Antiquarian Society, 1996

Snowdonia Aviation Historical Group, *The Air War Over Gwynedd*, 1985

Watkins, David, *De Havilland Vampire – The Complete History*, Sutton Publishing, 1996

Williams, Captain T.B., *Airship Pilot No.28*, William Kimber & Co., 1974

AVAILABLE FROM
GWASG CARREG GWALCH

- ## CIRCULAR WALKS ON ANGLESEY
  ISBN 0-86381-478-6; £4.50

- ## AN ANGLESEY ANTHOLOGY
  - Dewi Roberts. *ISBN 0-86381-566-9; £4.95*

- ## ANGLESEY PAST AND PRESENT
  Wendy Hughes. *ISBN 0-86381-560-X; £4.95*

- ## ANGLESEY SKETCHES
  - Margaret Hughes (with sketches by N. Squire Johnson).
  ISBN 0-86381-540-5; £3.95

- ## ANGLESEY – THE ISLAND' STORY
  - Michael Senior; 64 pp. *ISBN 0-86381-389-5; £2.75*

- ## TWO BRIDGES OVER MENAI
  - Robin Richards. History of the construction of the bridges across the Menai Straits.
  ISBN 0-86381-387-9; £2.75

- ## ANGLESEY REMEMBERS
  Eminent people of the island; *Margaret Hughes; ISBN: 0-86381-614-2; £4.75*

- ## ANGLESEY'S COASTAL FISHING TRADITION
  Mike Smylie; ISBN: 0-86381-615-0; £4.95

Available from
GWASG CARREG GWALCH
12 Iard yr Orsaf, Llanrwst, Dyffryn Conwy,
Cymru (Wales) LL26 0EH
☎ 01492 642031
01492 641502
e-bost/e-mail: books@carreg-gwalch.co.uk
lle ar y we/website: www.carreg-gwalch.co.uk